THE
TEMPEST

THE
TEMPEST

_____

WILLIAM SHAKESPEARE

INTRODUCTION
BY DR CHRIS MCNAB

This edition published in 2023 by Arcturus Publishing Limited
26/27 Bickels Yard, 151–153 Bermondsey Street,
London SE1 3HA

Typesetting by Sooky Choi

Cover design: Peter Ridley
Cover illustration: Paula Zamudio

AD010242UK

Printed in the UK

CONTENTS

CONTENTS

INTRODUCTION

———➤●◀———

Presentism is the doctrine, or rather unavoidable tendency, of seeing the past only through the eyes of present-day morals, norms and knowledge. When applied to Shakespeare's works, presentism labours under the illusion that if you were a citizen of Jacobean times, you would judge all that you see in the same way you do today. Yet while we can find voices from the past who chime with present views, it is a cognitive leap to say that our personality and moral framework would survive wholesale after transportation four centuries back in time to what was, in effect, a world foreign to the one we inhabit today.

Presentism is a temporal challenge when evaluating any Shakespeare play, and *The Tempest* is no exception. Take the following passage as a case in point. In Act II, scene ii, Trinculo the jester has his first encounter with Caliban, the enslaved creature on what is now Prospero's island. After the initial knockabout introduction, Trinculo objectifies Caliban with the most ebullient and empowered racism:

> I shall laugh myself to death at this puppy-
> headed monster. A most scurvy monster! I
> could find in my heart to beat him,—

II. ii. 158–160

For Trinculo, Caliban is a figure of nothing but derision, objectified in language that seems to dig down to rock-bottom of contempt. Note that Trinculo fuses laughter and violence in one unwholesome package, as if the only thing stopping Caliban becoming a punchbag is the energy Trinculo has already expended in mocking laughter.

For modern viewers, the lesson is clear – this is vile racism in full flow, rightly deserving of our condemnation. After all, the world has thankfully moved on. But the attempt to use our moral compass to navigate Shakespeare's 'message' for the seventeenth-century audience is more complex. Not least this is because the audience four centuries ago could have radically different takes on the relationship between cruelty and humour. For example, a significant percentage of the *same* audience for Shakespeare's plays would have also spent its time enthusiastically watching the spectacle of animal-baiting, in which a large animal (typically a bear or a bull) was tied to a stake and then attacked by a pack of fighting dogs, with resulting injury and/or death. Animal cruelty in those days was creatively diverse, including dogfights, cockfights, rat-baitings, monkey fights and beating blind animals. And note, this was not just low-end entertainment – both Queen Elizabeth and her successor, King James, were said to be fans of baiting.

Via contemporary first-hand accounts of these practices, we see that audiences often found the violence funny or celebratory in a way that today would probably be considered psychotic. In this world, cruelty *is* entertainment. The generalized enthusiasm for brutality also extended to people, in a range of public tortures and executions including methods that never fail to make chilling reading. So, if we are attempting to extract Shakespeare's moral judgement on the treatment of Caliban, our task becomes that much harder when we take into account the ambient cruelty of the day. In Shakespeare's time, deformity and 'exotic' ethnicities were profit-turning fairground attractions, not humanity to be understood. Of Caliban, Trinculo says that:

> Were I in
>
> England now [...]
>   there would this monster make
> a man; any strange beast there makes a man:
> when they will not give a doit to relieve a lame
> beggar, they will lay out ten to see a dead Indian

II. ii. 28–34

Trinculo is referring to the display of captured New World 'Indians' for entertainment and that there was good money to be had from doing so. Those unfortunate enough to be held in this state often died from the neglect, stress and mistreatment that came with it, but the owner would make the most of his investment by displaying the dead body, as Trinculo is aware. So, while we might see Shakespeare holding Trinculo up as a contemptible specimen, many of his audience (whom, we must acknowledge, he was keen to keep) would have seen both the logic and the entertainment in Trinculo's entrepreneurial vision. Put bluntly, for much of the audience there *was* comedy in Caliban, born partly of the sheer severity of the times, partly through ignorance, and partly through equating physical difference with moral baseness.

So is Shakespeare simply giving the crowd what they want in *The Tempest*? The answer, as ever with Shakespeare, seems more complex than that. One of his undeniable strengths as a playwright is that he effectively holds up a mirror to the audience, compelling them to examine what they do, think and say, often through challenges to their own preconceptions. Shakespeare provides the ingredients, not the answers, of self-analysis through the possibilities of character and plot. Hence directors of *The Tempest* to this day spend stimulating hours in debate with their actors, thrashing through the many possibilities of how characters should be played.

SOURCES AND STAGING

The first recorded performance of *The Tempest* was in 1611, at the court of King James (James I of England and Ireland and VI of Scotland). Notably, it is probably the last play written solely by Shakespeare himself. The three others credited to him but staged after *The Tempest* – *Cardenio* (later adapted as *Double Falsehood*), *Henry VIII* and *The Two Noble Kinsmen* – were either collaborations or have disputed provenance.

In terms of source material, *The Tempest* sits upon a collection of indirect influences rather than relying on a single narrative source. The enabling device of the play – storm and shipwreck – was a topical hard reality for the seafaring and increasingly colonial British. In the sixteenth and seventeenth centuries, approximately 25–30 per cent of oceanic voyages ended in fatal shipwreck. About 40 per cent of the causes of loss were not known – ships would just sail off, crest the horizon, then disappear – but some incidents became public headlines. A key source for *The Tempest* was the pamphlet (read as an unpublished manuscript by Shakespeare) *True Reportory of the Wrack* [Wreck], *and Redemption of Sir Thomas Gates Knight*, written by William Strachey in 1610. It recounted the story of a fleet of nine vessels that set out from England in 1609 with 500 colonists, destined for Jamestown settlement, Virginia. An Atlantic storm separated the flagship *The Sea Venture*, with future Virginia governor Sir Thomas Gates aboard, from the rest of the ships. *The Sea Venture* was subsequently wrecked on the shores of Bermuda. The crew not only survived, however, but thrived in a tropical haven replete with food and water. Yet what might have been a paradisical settlement was polluted by human faction and dispute, with some parallels to *The Tempest*. Indeed, Shakespeare extracted some detailed specifics from the *True Reportory*, such as an account of St Elmo's fire playing along the ship masts during the storm, a phenomenon deployed by Ariel to overawe the passengers and crew in *The Tempes*t:

> I flamed amazement: sometime I'ld divide,
> And burn in many places; on the topmast,

9

The yards and bowsprit, would I flame distinctly,
Then meet and join.

I. ii. 198–201

The Tempest was written in what we now call the 'Age of Discovery', when the European maritime powers began exploring and colonizing the world in earnest, with Britain leaning outwards to the Americas, Caribbean and West Africa. Trans-oceanic exploration brought the British into contact with peoples and cultures that were utterly foreign, alien even – to an extent we today can scarcely appreciate.

Such was the comparative strangeness of the foreign lands that it is little wonder the British public lapped up a sensational diet of monsters, hybrid human-animals, opulent nature and sadistic barbarity – the wide world became a blank sheet upon which the Europeans projected their fantasies and nightmares. But there were those who took a more contemplative view, and who exerted further influence upon *The Tempest*. Michel de Montaigne's *Des Cannibales* (*The Cannibals*), translated into English in 1603, was partly an anthropological study of cannibalistic Brazilian peoples, but also a challenge to 'civilized' society to contemplate its own plentiful cruelties before coming to judgement on others. Montaigne argued the case for what became known later in the century as the 'noble savage', a native figure who may have been unsophisticated by European models, but who carried innocence and natural simplicity, free from the internecine guile, political tortures and rolling wars of the West. We perhaps trace Montaigne's influence on the play in the moral jousting between Prospero and Caliban, the latter, as we shall see, asserting his human dignity against the values of an outsider.

Regarding other sources, Ovid's *Metamorphoses* offered Shakespeare some mythical archetypes for characters such as Prospero and Ariel. By contrast, a contemporary of Shakespeare – the famous mathematician, astronomer, occultist and alchemist John Dee – is also perceived as a model for the character of Prospero, an individual whose bookish learning takes him into magical realms. Our modern world's absolute division between science and the supernatural was acceptably blurred back in Shakespeare's day; in a world infused by divine fiat and capricious spirits, rational investigation could lead into more esoteric realms quite comfortably.

Upon the specific sources of inspiration behind *The Tempest*, we can also layer the generalized influence of the comedic genre, crafted around tropes such as exotic settings, characters in disguise, convoluted subplots and, above all, marriage – the point at which all the comedic lines naturally converge.

PLOT SUMMARY AND CHARACTERS

Act I, scene i opens the play aboard a storm-wracked ship, fighting for survival in terrifying seas. It is noteworthy that the tempest to be evoked on stage lends the play its title. In the Renaissance imagination, powerful storms were held to be more than mere climatic events. Rather they could be seen as sympathetic reflections of great spiritual fractures, turmoil in the affairs of humanity made manifest in wind, lightning, thunder and rain. There is governing power in the storm – in *The Tempest* it is the foundation on which all that follows is built.

In the opening scene we meet two of the ship's crew – the Master and the Boatswain, both struggling to save the ship – plus members of a royal party: Alonso, the king of Naples; his brother Sebastian; Ferdinand, the son of Alonso; Antonio, the usurping Duke of Milan (brother of Prospero); Gonzalo, an ageing and trusted counsellor to the king; and two lords, Adrian and Francisco. Later in the play, it is revealed that the party are returning from Tunis, having attended the wedding of Alonso's daughter, Claribel, to the king of Tunisia. The fact that Claribel has married a non-European would have been noted by the contemporary audience, and indeed later becomes a criticism directed against Alonso by Sebastian. For now, however, the drama concentrates on the struggle against the elements and the clashes between the frightened courtiers and the overworked mariners. The boatswain's job is made more difficult by noble interference, and in return he is judged on his class and his appearance. Gonzalo notes how the man seems destined for the death of a criminal: 'methinks he hath no drowning mark upon him; / his complexion is perfect gallows' (I. i. 31–32). Yet Shakespeare, doubtless aware of the tiers of society attending the play, also playfully subverts class divisions. The boatswain sees no competence or benefit in noble passengers, noting to Gonzalo that in the face of the storm all are equally powerless and that self-preservation takes precedence over propriety:

> Gon.   Good, yet remember whom thou hast
>   aboard.
> Boats.   None that I more love than myself. You
>   are a counsellor; if you can command these
>   elements to silence
>
> I. i. 20–24

As the vessel appears doomed to destruction, the passengers are finally compelled to abandon ship and swim to shore, an act that divides them into several separate parties in the process.

In **Act I, scene ii**, the drama moves from shore to land, the setting now a mystical island. As with plays such as *Othello*, which sets most of its drama on Cyprus, the use of an island environment signifies a special domain, a truly 'foreign' setting isolated from norms of nature and society. On this island we now meet Prospero, the former duke of Milan, and his teenage daughter Miranda, who arrived on the island with her father at the age of three. In the opening lines of the scene, she makes it clear that the storm offshore has been summoned by her father's magical powers – he has taken control of the elements for purposes yet to be divined by the audience. Miranda appears as gentle and humane, fretting for the wellbeing of the sailors and passengers at sea, while Prospero reassures her that all will be safe. He now deems it time, however, for her to hear how she and her father came to be on the island.

Prospero recounts how he was formerly the Duke of Milan and she his infant princess. He confesses that he neglected the many duties of state in preference for eyes-down intellectual study, hinting that his interests lay particularly in the magical arts. His head in books, Prospero effectively delegated rule to his brother Antonio, who soon discovered an appetite for power. Surreptitiously and skilfully, he put in place the architecture for a coup, turning Milan's influential citizens against their duke. Prospero explains his manoeuvres in terms of a spreading parasitic infection, weakening his position:

> now he was
> The ivy which had hid my princely trunk,
> And suck'd my verdure out on 't

I. ii. 85–87

Antonio's final move before checkmate was to approach Alonso of Naples and offer to pay him an annual tribute if he assisted in the deposition of Prospero. Alonso assented and, in the final acts of the coup, even sent an army to assist in the night-time overthrow. Prospero was forcibly removed from office, but to avoid a backlash from Milan's citizens neither he nor Miranda was killed. Instead, father and daughter were set adrift in a rotting boat, the plotters expecting both to die at sea. They were saved, however, by Gonzalo, who provided the pair with food, water, clothing and, crucially, many of Prospero's books, clearly of future significance to Prospero:

> Knowing I loved my books, he furnish'd me
> From mine own library with volumes that
> I prize above my dukedom.

I. ii. 166–168

Books have an unusual level of influence in *The Tempest*. On the one hand, they are for Prospero the distracting source of his political downfall, a fact he himself admits. But the learning contained in the books, especially in terms of the magical arts, will be the very thing that enables him to restore his power, both over the island and its inhabitants and ultimately over Milan.

Prospero now outlines his current plans. He explains that he has deliberately brought 'mine enemies' (I. ii. 179) to the island, engineering the events to take advantage of auspicious astrological alignments. With the situation explained, Prospero then sends Miranda into a magically induced slumber.

The scene so far establishes Prospero as a loving, protective father, albeit one who has acquired extraordinary powers. As further island characters are introduced, however, the play offers broadening room for interpretation of his character. Ariel, Prospero's magical spirit servant, now enters. The great storm offshore has largely been Ariel's work, at Prospero's command, the sprite orchestrating the lightning and waves to separate the king's ship from the rest of the fleet and to split the evacuated party into sub-groups. An exception is the king's son, Ferdinand, who has made landfall on his own and now walks the island alone in the belief that his father has drowned. Ariel reassures Prospero that the mariners are still safe aboard the ship, which rests in port having stayed afloat after all.

The exchange between the two reinforces the impression of Prospero wielding near omnipotence over events, fine-tuning the details of circumstance. Ariel proudly confirms that he has performed his duties 'To every article' (I. ii. 195), while Prospero acknowledges 'Ariel, thy charge/ Exactly is perform'd' (I. ii. 237–238). But when Prospero says that he expects more service from Ariel, the tensions emerge. Ariel reminds Prospero that the ultimate outcome of their contractual arrangement is that he will be freed from servitude:

> Remember I have done thee worthy service;
> Told thee no lies, made thee no mistakings, served
> Without or grudge or grumblings: thou didst promise
> To bate me a full year.

I. ii. 247–250

Behind the explanation, Ariel is effectively accusing Prospero of keeping him climbing ever upwards towards liberty, but forever being confounded by false summits. This will not be the first time the justice of Prospero's rule over the island's inhabitants will be challenged. A director faces key character choices at this point. Is Prospero to be depicted as a tyrant, towering over a trembling Ariel, or is Ariel to be defiant and angry, chipping away justly at Prospero's weakening rule?

Following Ariel's challenge, Prospero's main response is guilt-imposing anger. He reminds Ariel whence he came, something he apparently has to do on a monthly basis (evidently this is a persistent thorn in the side of their relationship). Prospero recounts how the witch Sycorax, while pregnant, was banished to the island from Algiers (pregnant witches were spared execution). On the island she gave birth to 'A freckled whelp hag-born—not honour'd with / A human shape' (I. ii. 283–284) – this child is Caliban. Ariel became her servant, but because he defied some of her devilish instructions she imprisoned him within the trunk of a pine tree, leaving him locked in immobile agony for 12 years. During this time, Sycorax died and Prospero arrived, finding and freeing Ariel but binding the spirit into indebted servitude, promising eventual liberty. Prospero clearly sees Ariel's service in a master–slave framework, threatening to return him to an arboreal nightmare – imprisonment in an oak tree – if he keeps complaining. At this threat, Ariel is once again cowed into obedience, but his legitimate resistance registers with Prospero, who promises that in return for just two more days of service he will be set free.

Ariel now exits and Miranda is awakened, going with her father to visit Caliban. To modern audiences, there follows one of the more unpleasant episodes in the play. Caliban, presented as some sort of hybrid human/monster, has evidently become Prospero's slave in the fullest sense, as Prospero outlines his duties:

> he does make our fire,
> Fetch in our wood, and serves in offices
> That profit us. What, ho! slave! Caliban!
> Thou earth, thou! speak.

I. ii. 311–314

Caliban may be enslaved, but he is passionately resistant, his very first words in the play hurling defiance at Prospero:

> As wicked dew as e'er my mother brush'd
> With raven's feather from unwholesome fen
> Drop on you both! a south-west blow on ye
> And blister you all o'er!

I. ii. 321–324

Prospero responds by saying the penalty for these words will be night-time visitations from bodily pain and tormenting spirits – clearly, physical coercion rather than respectful compliance is the root of his dominance over Caliban. Plaintively, Caliban outlines his history for both Prospero and the audience. He tells how after the death of his mother he became the ruler of the island. Then Prospero and Miranda arrived. At first, Caliban was treated civilly by Prospero, giving him a formal education. In return, Caliban gave Prospero insight into the parts and nature of the island, and how to thrive there. But eventually Prospero 'takest from me' (I. ii. 332) the island, enslaving Caliban with his magically backed powers. Prospero pushes back against the accusations vehemently, claiming that he effectively dragged Caliban out of a brutish state, expressed most contemptibly by Caliban's attempt to rape Miranda. Prospero's position is that he initially treated Caliban respectfully, but Caliban's innate savagery took over, despite the civilization that Prospero attempted to impart.

It is an uncomfortable scene, with seesawing sympathies and arguments, all underwritten by an ingrained contempt for Caliban. A subdued Caliban exits.

The lengthy scene continues with a switch to Ferdinand, wandering alone across the island. An invisible Ariel uses an enchanted song to steer his direction, Ferdinand reflecting that one of the songs reminds him of his father's death at sea. Ariel eventually leads Ferdinand to Miranda and Prospero. The two young people have an express attraction for one another, Ferdinand even thinking that he has arrived in the presence of a goddess. To Prospero – who is fully cognizant of Ferdinand's identity – Ferdinand presents himself as the King of Naples, accepting this as his position following the death of his father. He also puts his foot on the gas regarding romance, declaring his desire to make Miranda his queen.

This section of the play is punctuated by numerous asides to the audience – Miranda commenting about the strange manner of her father's interactions with Ferdinand, Prospero speaking to Ariel about purposes yet to come, and to the audience about his intention to put obstacles in the path of the courtship, to test its sincerity. Although Prospero has much control, it is clear that the marriage is not predestinate. In Shakespearean comedies, the vagaries and wilfulness of romantic love form the source energy of much of the drama – the path to marriage cannot be a certitude or the comedy is deprived of its drive.

During his discussion with Ferdinand, Prospero works up a confrontation, provoking Ferdinand to draw his sword in anger. In response, Prospero freezes him motionless. Miranda, clearly as besotted with Ferdinand as he with her, defends him and pleads his case. Prospero eventually releases Ferdinand from the spell, but Ferdinand understands that he is now effectively a prisoner, trapped on the island under the power of Prospero, but also in thrall to his new-found love. Here Ferdinand intersects with a core theme of *The Tempest*, that of enslavement, and the degree to which those enslaved are culpable for their fate, or not. But because Ferdinand has found love, he sees his exile on the island as an inversion of slavery, a freedom within his subjugation:

> Might I but through my prison once a day
> Behold this maid: all comers else o' th' earth
> Let liberty make use of; space enough
> Have I in such a prison.

I. ii. 490–494

The Tempest plays with the question of what is a justifiable, indeed bearable, slavery. It also asks, *What is the right of one to control the freedom of another?* We will return to these questions below, but for Ferdinand servitude has become the space of love's liberty, because that is all he now desires. Like Ariel, however, Ferdinand has freedom on the horizon, a liberation from his labours through eventual marriage.

Act II, scene i shifts the action to another part of the island, where we find Alonso and his entourage negotiating their precipitous change in fortune. The scene provides deeper character revelations within the royal party and the divisions hidden beneath the formality. Alonso is stricken with depression and demotivation at the loss of his son. The ever-faithful Gonzalo once again demonstrates his glass-half-full mentality, seeking to lift Alonso's spirits by pointing to the very miracle of their survival. In the scene, Gonzalo also sermonizes on the idyllic potential of the island, which to him offers a blank sheet upon which the mythological Golden Age could be reinvented, building a utopian commonwealth free from poverty and excess, crime and violence, hunger and division.

Gonzalo's optimistic and good-natured musings are, however, punctuated and undermined by constant snide exchanges between Sebastian and Antonio. On one level, they are making a comedic contribution, puncturing idealism and pontification. The two men come across as sharp-witted and funny, but at the same time they are callous and without empathy, mocking Gonzalo's transparent goodness and disconnected from Alonso's grief. In fact, they add to the king's mental burdens, questioning the prudence of the arranged marriage between Claribel and the king of Tunisia. Sebastian even attributes the death of Ferdinand and their present predicament to the breaking of racial and cultural boundaries in the marriage:

> Sir, you may thank yourself for this great loss,
> That would not bless our Europe with your daughter,
> But rather lose her to an African;

Where she, at least, is banish'd from your eye,
Who hath cause to wet the grief on 't

II. i. 123–127

The racial theme is key to *The Tempest*. Shakespeare's European characters often view foreigners with outright racism at worst or suspicion of their otherness at best, but in plays such as *Othello* and *The Merchant of Venice* Shakespeare gives foreign characters the voice to make at least some defence of their dignity and circumstances. Beyond their attack, however, Sebastian and Antonio also compare the marriage to the Greek myth of Dido and Aeneas (as written by Virgil in the *Aeneid*) – a great love but one in which Dido is ultimately betrayed and commits suicide in despair.

Ariel enters unseen and uses his magic to send all to sleep apart from Sebastian and Antonio, who are now free to talk and plot. Antonio, a man already proven capable of ruthless ambition, goes to work on Sebastian. He convinces him to murder his father as he sleeps, the prize being the crown of Naples. Sebastian is seduced by the plan and stimulates it further by asking Antonio to kill Alonso while he simultaneously murders Gonzalo, also assuring Antonio that his assistance in the killings will be rewarded by cancelling the tribute that Milan currently pays to Naples.

The Tempest is now a darkening play, the scene showing the Machiavellian instincts thriving at the heart of the Italian court. Antonio gives vain credence to his plan by asking Sebastian to contemplate how well the garb of ducal office suits him since he usurped his brother's position, to which Sebastian enquires about the restraints of conscience. Antonio's dismissive reply speaks volumes:

Ay, sir; where lies that? if 'twere a kibe,
'T would put me to my slipper: but I feel not
This deity in my bosom: twenty consciences,
That stand 'twixt me and Milan, candied be they,
And melt, ere they molest!

II. i. 276–280

Antonio's conscience is irrelevant and malfunctioning, an impediment to action dismissed as if it were an unwanted sweet melting away to nothing.

The two men build up to act, drawing and raising their swords. Ariel now enters, Prospero having correctly foretold Alonso's danger, and wakes Alonso and the others before the assassins have time to strike. The two would-be murderers excuse their drawn weapons by saying they were protecting the sleepers from wild animals. They are believed, albeit thwarted, and the party sets off to search for the body of Ferdinand.

In **Act II, scene ii**, the scene moves again to a different part of the island. We see Caliban labouring bitterly, bearing his loads and duties with part defiance, part fear – he is always aware that Prospero's collaborating spirits are watching him. Caliban then spots Trinculo, Alonso's court jester, landing on the nearby coast. Fearing that Trinculo is another of Prospero's tormenting spirits, he hides under his cloak on the ground. Trinculo enters. He is a coarse, rambling, extravagant and foolish character, and the action is now played for laughs. He spots the lumpen cloak and recognizes that there is a man beneath it (at first, he thinks Caliban is some form of fish). Seeking shelter from impending bad weather, Trinculo crawls beneath the cloak.

At this point Stephano, a 'drunken butler' according to the *dramatis personae*, enters. He is a habitual drunk, having appropriately floated ashore from the shipwreck on a barrel of wine. He spots the now four-legged cloak and through his drink-clouded brain imagines that it is some chimeric animal. Farcical comedy ensures as Stephano interacts with the creature, eventually unveiling the two men hiding within. The action is replete with puns, physical humour, sexual references and proverbial allusions; the scene is scripted for humour above all. Yet as ever, there is a darker side. Like Prospero, both Stephano and Trinculo make numerous bullying jabs at Caliban. Stephano defines him as a 'moon-calf' (II. ii. 111), a reference to a deformed animal born under the full moon, an aberration from nature.

Caliban is afraid of the two men, seeing them as possible supernatural visitors, and attempts to placate them by showing them around the island. He is introduced to alcohol, however, and quickly descends into drunkenness. (Stories regarding the ease with which native peoples became drunk were another twisted source of amusement for contemporary audiences.) In his lubricated state, Caliban elevates Stephano to the status of a god for worship. Feeling defiant, he renounces his servitude to Prospero and transfers his allegiance to Stephano, seeing this in terms of a liberation from slavery rather than a continuation of it.

Act III, scene i brings us back to the two young lovers, Ferdinand and Miranda. The scene is infused with rose-coloured romance but set against Prospero's dictates. Ferdinand is performing hard labour as imposed by Prospero, the physical effort ostensibly to tease out any insincerity in Ferdinand's love proclamations. Ferdinand, mindful of Miranda's concern for his wellbeing, explains that present struggles are inconsequential compared to the eventual joy that will come from their marriage. The theatre-going Jacobean audience would have been familiar with the depiction of lovers overcoming trials prior to marriage; it was a central trope of the comedic genre. Prospero's dictates would likely be seen more as warranted parental testing rather than petty interference.

Shakespeare's age sits at the intersection of two different attitudes to marriage. First, marriage could be a strategic and economic arrangement, with romantic love a pleasant offshoot but not required. Second, marriage was the expression of burgeoning spiritual love, a power that was capable of overriding convention and even propriety. The second of these approaches was more individualistic, but in some ways had a higher risk – real love could be masked by artifice and lust, so needed testing. Ferdinand confesses to Miranda that he has previously been attracted to many ladies, but 'some defect' (III. i. 44) in them blocked flowering relationships, whereas he sees Miranda as perfect in every regard. Miranda responds by explaining that she has never seen other women as a frame of comparison. This response only adds to her innocent appeal. Notably, the scene ends with Ferdinand offering Miranda his hand, effectively a formal commitment to marriage.

For all its tenderness, the scene is made a little more awkward for the modern audience by the fact that Prospero watches it throughout, hidden on the sidelines and commenting on what he witnesses. He nonetheless evidently approves of the union, not least because it is a key piece of the jigsaw in his overarching scheme.

In **Act III, scene ii**, we return to the clattering company of Stephano, Trinculo and Caliban, this time accompanied by the invisible, mischievous presence of Ariel. Caliban remains the butt of caustic, racist jokes. Trinculo evidently holds Caliban in distaste, and suspects his motives. Ariel capitalizes on this, impersonating Trinculo's voice and causing both Stephano and Caliban to turn on him – at one point Stephano even beats Trinculo. Caliban is given the opportunity to explain more of his history and how Prospero robbed him of freedom through sorcery. He then lays out a plot for his new confidantes. He calls for them first to steal and burn Prospero's books – the physical source of his spiritual powers – then kill him. In return, he promises to give Miranda to Stephano as his breeding wife. Stephano assents to the plan.

Again, to modern eyes this whole scene is frequently distasteful, although the drunkenness involved means it can be played for laughs. Caliban is dehumanized constantly, referred to frequently as 'monster' and in other derogatory though less direct terms. But at the same time, Shakespeare gives him enough of a voice to hint at the potential justice of his cause.

In **Act III, scene iii**, we are once more with Alonso and the royal entourage. Alonso and Gonzalo are weary from their journey, and Antonio and Sebastian see in their beckoning drowsiness an opportunity to perform the killings. In a strange supernatural turn, however, Prospero enters to ethereal music (although unrecognized by the others) and summons his spirits to conjure up a magical feast before the hungry men. The onlookers speculate about the otherworldly sight, but when they go to eat Ariel appears as a harpy (half woman, half taloned bird), spirits the feast away and delivers a lengthy condemnation of the onlookers. He calls down curses and imprecations while also challenging them directly about their part in the overthrow and exile of Prospero. His message delivered, he vanishes. Prospero lauds Ariel's performance and sees the moral noose tightening around the group:

> My high charms work,
> And these mine enemies are all knit up
> In their distractions: they now are in my power

III. iii. 88–90

By this stage of the play, we start to see Prospero as a heightened choreographer of the other characters. Certainly, Alonso now feels his guilt laid bare, his thoughts turning suicidal:

> The name of Prosper: it did bass my trespass.
> Therefore my son i' th' ooze is bedded; and
> I'll seek him deeper than e'er plummet sounded,
> And with him there lie mudded.

III. iii. 99–102

While Alonso sees drowning as a way to smother his grief and despair, Sebastian and Antonio, by contrast, stick with their plan, looking to fight the spirits rather than defer to them.

Act IV, scene i, set in front of Prospero's cell, opens with Ferdinand and Prospero in discussion. Prospero softens his position towards Ferdinand and consents to the marriage, albeit balanced with some rather fearful judgements about what will happen if Ferdinand attempts to take Miranda's virginity before completion of the marriage rites. Again we encounter one of the more provocative aspects of Prospero's character, the way he runs punitive anger alongside benign contemplation. It is an open question as to where the fulcrum of his personality lies.

Ariel enters. Prospero tells him to bring the 'rabble' (IV. i. 37) – i.e. the royal party – to them. In the meantime, Prospero says he will use his powers to stir up a spectacle for the lovers, before again giving a final warning to Ferdinand about reining in his lust. His commands in this regard appear as more than just parental squeamishness. He hints at the dire consequences of defying his order, as if the chain of events Prospero has set in play remains a house of cards that could brought down by a single incongruent action.

Ariel exits and Prospero stirs up an otherworldly pageant of Greek and Roman gods and goddess. The display follows the Renaissance tradition of the masque, an event in which masked participants make a ceremonial gift-giving procession, accompanied by music, drama and dance and often organized around an allegorical or mythological theme. According to Iris, the goddess of the rainbow, the divine masque in *The Tempest* is:

> A contract of true love to celebrate;
> And some donation freely to estate
> On the blest lovers
>
> IV. i. 84–86

True to its purpose, the masque cycles through many of the great Graeco-Roman divinities, each bearing a message for the lovers, often revolving around themes of fertility. But in a notable exchange between Prospero and Ferdinand, the magician somewhat qualifies the authority of his creation:

> *Fer.*   This is a most majestic vision, and
> Harmonious charmingly. May I be bold
> To think these spirits?
> *Pros.*   Spirits, which by mine art
> I have from their confines call'd to enact
> My present fancies.
>
> IV. i. 118–122

Prospero suggests that what Ferdinand sees is a reification of Prospero's inner desires, a projector screen playing with the images of his own psychology and a dream-like landscape of passing authority. This point is generalized in one of the most famous passages in Shakespeare, in which Prospero confesses that the display is mere theatre, ephemeral and fleeting, providing a metaphor for human existence itself:

> We are such stuff
> As dreams are made on; and our little life
> Is rounded with a sleep.
>
> IV. i. 156–158

This suggests that what we see as concrete about reality might in fact be just fleeting dreams, set between the voids of non-existence.

Prospero finally disperses the masque and remembers that Caliban, Stephano and Trinculo all need his attention. Ariel tells Prospero that he has led the group with siren-like song into a foul swamp, where they are trapped. Prospero vents his intention to punish them, although considering Caliban to be beyond the pale of moral redemption.

At this point Prospero and Ariel, both now invisible, watch the comically ineffectual actions of the three men, a magnificently incapable group. Prospero has instructed Ariel to hang many fine clothes on a line to distract Stephano and Trinculo from their purpose. The device works to perfection. While Caliban retains a laser-like focus on killing Prospero, his drunk and deflected confederates are drawn to the clothes like magpies to shiny objects. They quickly forget the plan, deck themselves out ludicrously in the clothing and swagger, much to Caliban's disgust. Then Prospero unleashes a pack of spirit dogs, driving the incompetent trio from the scene.

Act V, scene i is the penultimate scene of the play, the point at which the moral snares laid by Prospero are finally primed. The royal party are trapped by Ariel's magic in a lime-tree grove. Prospero orders Ariel to release them and bring them to his cell. Notably, Ariel tells Prospero that the group are truly dejected from their ordeal, so it is advisable to soften his harshness. Prospero agrees, mollifying his attitude:

> Yet with my nobler reason 'gainst my fury
> Do I take part: the rarer action is
> In virtue than in vengeance: they being penitent,
> The sole drift of my purpose doth extend
> Not a frown further.

> V. i. 26–30

The relaxation of mood builds the sense that his project may be nearing fulfilment and acts of release – Alonso from grief, Miranda from romantic isolation, Ariel from servitude, and Prospero himself from exile. Prospero also reaches this insight: that when all is done, he will have no more need for conjuring powers. Thus when Ariel exits, Prospero makes a long incantation to the spirits, pledging that when all falls into place he'll destroy the instruments of magic:

> I'll break my staff,
> Bury it certain fathoms in the earth,
> And deeper than did ever plummet sound
> I'll drown my book.

> V. i. 54–57

This statement of intent makes it clear that Prospero's magic is bound up with practices as much educational as spiritual, hence the source connection between Prospero and the occultist John Dee.

The royal group now enter and Ariel helps Prospero dress for his great reveal; Prospero also tenderly promises Ariel that his freedom is near. Finally, Prospero presents himself to the bewildered, then remorseful, group. He lays down fierce castigation upon Alonso, Sebastian and Antonio, but he also extends forgiveness and reconciliation. He tells Alonso that he has also 'lost' a child, but then reveals his true meaning by showing Ferdinand and Miranda together, playing chess. Alonso is joyous at the reunification with his living son and celebrates the betrothal, but also feels guilt over his historical treatment of Prospero. Prospero seeks to lift all eyes upward, releasing the tension for both characters and audience:

> Let us not burthen our remembrances with
> A heaviness that's gone.

> V. i. 199–200

Ariel enters with the Master and the Boatswain. They inform everyone that the ship is fit to sail back to Italy. While Alonso wonders at the strange turn in events, Prospero instructs Ariel to break Stephano and Trinculo out of their ludicrous infatuation with their new clothes, and present them and Caliban before him. The three men are ultimately contrite, with Caliban accepting how foolish it was to follow the drunken Stephano:

> I'll be wise hereafter,
> And seek for grace. What a thrice-double ass
> Was I, to take this drunkard for a god,
> And worship this dull fool!

> V. i. 294–297

Much is swept under the carpet here, not least the suggestion that the only reason Caliban didn't follow through with Prospero's killing was that he paired himself with idiots.

But all is now well. Prospero tells the listeners that they will retire to his cell, where he can recount what happened since his exile, and then they will sail to Naples to enact the marriage of Ferdinand and Miranda, after which his dukedom will be restored in Milan.

The Tempest ends with a famous **Epilogue**. Prospero gently addresses the audience directly, explaining that his magic is now gone and asking them to free him from the stage with their applause. Across time, many have seen the Epilogue as Shakespeare's direct voice, asking the audience to bring down the curtain on his long career. This position is questionable (see below), but it certainly brings *The Tempest* to a complete, self-reflexive ending.

POWER, CIVILIZATION AND SLAVERY IN
THE TEMPEST

The Tempest is a play soaked in the exoticism of the Age of Discovery. Through the prism of both real exploration and popular imagination, the seventeenth century was a period in which distant horizons were brought closer through adventurism and commerce, producing encounters with people and lands beyond the often stolid limits of British imagination. Exploration of the wider world both magnetized and appalled, a tension investigated within the play.

The action is set on an unknown island between Italy and North Africa, but Shakespeare infuses the setting with elements well beyond the Mediterranean. For example, Caliban refers to the 'nimble marmoset' (II. ii. 174) – actually an animal brought to Europe from Brazil – and his sorceress mother, Sycorax, is said to be a worshipper of Setebos, a Patagonian deity. The play contains several other references and allusions to the Americas, an exporter of many of the stories of adventure regaling British society. But the geographic waywardness of the island is not important. What matters, rather, is the confrontation between European characters and the otherness of foreign lands, the clash between 'civilization' and the fantastical.

The Tempest has gone through a shifting performative and critical context over its four-century history. Summarizing broadly, the focus during much of its staging journey has been on presenting Prospero as a temperamental but largely benevolent and just ruler over the island, bringing some order and shape to an untamed people (represented by Caliban) and a wild land. This interpretation ran hand in hand with the actual historical unfolding of British colonization, the expansion of an empire that was to cover about 25 per cent of the world's landmass.

There is plenty of ammunition within the play to arm this viewpoint. Prospero in effect colonizes the island (albeit in his own name rather than than that of a foreign state) and subjugates Caliban through civilizing effort and magical force of arms. Caliban's very name evokes the word 'cannibal', a subject of perennial fascination, lurid accounts of which were flowing back into Europe in exploration narratives and sensationalist illustrations. In argument with Caliban, Prospero makes clear that before he took over the island, he attempted to extend the hand of civilization to save Caliban from his own savagery:

> I pitied thee,
> Took pains to make thee speak, taught thee each hour

> One thing or other: when thou didst not, savage,
> Know thine own meaning, but wouldst gabble like
> A thing most brutish, I endow'd thy purposes
> With words that made them known. But thy vile race,
> Though thou didst learn, had that in 't which good natures
> Could not abide to be with
>
> I. ii. 353–360

We know already what prompted Prospero's change of heart and the contempt he now feels: Caliban's attempted rape of Miranda. This also explains why Miranda is disgusted by Caliban and his physical appearance, which she finds repulsive: "'Tis a villain, sir, / I do not love to look on' (I. ii. 309–310). Both are responses that no audience will begrudge. There are two points to note, however. First, that the shock for Shakespeare's early audiences will have included shock at the attempted violation of a European by a savage. Second that Caliban's precise physical form is not actually delineated in the play; the closest indication comes from the *dramatis personae*, which lists him as a 'savage and deformed Slave'. It is difficult to know, therefore, whether we should share the disgust Miranda naturally feels. As we witnessed in the plot summary and commentary, Caliban hunkers under downpours of debasing language, classifying him as both an animal and a commodity. Even drunks like Stephano and Trinculo are able to take positions of power, despite all their evident moral failings.

The critical scales began to tip more in Caliban's favour in the years after World War II, partly as decolonization provided space to question imperial legacies and establish more nuanced and ethical anthropologies, but also as non-European countries began exploring their own stagings of the play. Many now saw the subjugation of Caliban in its historical light, but also claimed his spirit of resistance, Shakespeare granting him enough voice and space to argue his case. By Caliban's account, he loved Prospero at first, the two men interacting with consideration and mutual respect. In return for Prospero's education, Caliban offered his own form of civilization – knowledge of an unfamiliar land, something that colonizers needed to acquire quickly if they were to survive. That value was lost the moment his relationship with Prospero broke down, and while we can understand the reason, what we see before us now is naked power:

> [I] show'd thee all the qualities o' th' isle,
> The fresh springs, brine-pits, barren place and fertile:
> Cursed be I that did so! All the charms
> Of Sycorax, toads, beetles, bats, light on you!
> For I am all the subjects that you have,

Which first was mine own king: and here you sty me
In this hard rock, whiles you do keep from me
The rest o' th' island.

I. ii. 337–344

The phrase 'mine own king' is paramount here. It raises issues about the right to rule and the justice of outsiders to impose their authority. Furthermore, Caliban questions whether European civility is just an ornate mask, concealing more base appetites and predatory behaviours. For example, in response to Prospero's argument that he gave Caliban the power of cultured language, Caliban points out the corruption within that gift:

You taught me language; and my profit on 't
Is, I know how to curse. The red plague rid you
For learning me your language!

I. ii. 363–365

What is important in this instance is not the sense that Prospero provided Caliban with a selection of juicy swear words, but more that Caliban received the conceptual framework of profanity. Essentially, Prospero imports a form of corruption into the island through the very linguistic framework of the colonizer.

Here Montaigne's arguments are starting to creep in, exposing something of the fallacy of the 'civilized' Europeans. That idea takes repeated knocks from the actual behaviour of the Europeans as they arrive from the shipwreck. Most of the characters in the play have little in the way of redeeming virtues – Antonio schemed in the overthrow of his own brother, and Alonso assisted; Sebastian plots the murder of his brother Alonso, aided by Antonio; Stephano and Trinculo are largely wasters with an appetite for drink and casually contemplated violence. Collectively, the Europeans present a parade of greed and vice. Gonzalo stands apart and it is notable how he is the one to envision an idyllic 'brave new world' (V. i. 183) – to repurpose Miranda's later term – one aired clear of civilization's thick smog of deceit, cruelty and greed. Ferdinand and Miranda also represent some hope for humanity, bottled in their love, although they are somewhat stock characters, providing a soft counterweight to the heavy corruption of others.

Shakespeare does not give either side in the 'civilization vs noble savage' debate a clean run to a winning argument. We reconnect here with the dangers of presentism outlined above. Perhaps there is no single message because there wasn't one at the time, just competing justifications with merit to weigh in argument, but which didn't ultimately affect the pragmatics of exploration and colonization. But this openness has given directors and actors a more unbounded landscape to explore, making decisions about tone, emphasis, posture, clothing, pace and other dramatic decisions which by themselves can transform the presentation of the characters and our interpretation of them.

PROSPERO AS PLAYWRIGHT

Over the centuries, *The Tempest* has held out a teasing possibility for literary critics and Shakespeare enthusiasts, namely that Prospero is Shakespeare, speaking to his audience and reflecting on his art even as the sun set over his career. In this view, Prospero is a valedictory mouthpiece for the bard himself.

The case largely rests upon seeing Prospero not purely as a potent sorcerer, but also as a playwright, tightly scripting the action of the drama around him and using theatrical devices – masques, sudden changes of scene, special effects, characters – to achieve his aims. We can also point to several moments in the play when Prospero reflects directly upon his machinations as a form of theatrical work. The first significant instance of this occurs in Act IV, scene i, when the spectral masque Prospero has created suddenly evaporates at his direction, giving way to a speech among the canon of great Shakespearean lines:

> Our revels now are ended. These our actors,
> As I foretold you, were all spirits, and
> Are melted into air, into thin air:
> And, like the baseless fabric of this vision,
> The cloud-capp'd towers, the gorgeous palaces,
> The solemn temples, the great globe itself,
> Yea, all which it inherit, shall dissolve,
> And, like this insubstantial pageant faded,
> Leave not a rack behind. We are such stuff
> As dreams are made on; and our little life
> Is rounded with a sleep.

IV. i. 148–158

Here Prospero unmasks the illusion of his art, revealing that what they have just witnessed is a matter of 'actors' and fleeting sets; the 'great globe' reference also evokes the Globe Theatre. There is a lament here: despite the grandeur of the show, it is a spectacle that is just temporary, in terms of both the duration of the play and the life of the playwright.

The second passage to back the view of Prospero as playwright, also enshrined in Shakespearean lore, comes from the Epilogue:

> But release me from my bands
> With the help of your good hands:
> Gentle breath of yours my sails
> Must fill, or else my project fails,
> Which was to please. Now I want
> Spirits to enforce, art to enchant;
> And my ending is despair,
> Unless I be relieved by prayer,
> Which pierces so, that it assaults
> Mercy itself, and frees all faults.
> As you from crimes would pardon'd be,
> Let your indulgence set me free.

Epilogue 9–20

Here Prospero decisively breaks the fourth wall. There is an implicit plea for the audience to appreciate the effort required to create the drama, an effort from which Prospero needs release, achieved through final applause. 'Set me free' evokes a sense of imprisonment within the drama. If we take the argument that Prospero is no less than Shakespeare, perhaps this line is a yearning for retirement, even the release of death.

Like Shakespeare, Prospero has had to work at his choreography and stagecraft. The detailed stage directions in *The Tempest* require special-effects machinery and skill to create illusions, much as Prospero must summon the dark arts in a mechanistic way to achieve his goals. For example, take this stage direction in Act III, scene iii (after line 52), an instruction to make Prospero's magical masque disappear:

> *Thunder and lightning. Enter Ariel, like a harpy; claps*
> *his wings upon the table; and, with a quaint device,*
> *the banquet vanishes.*

The 'quaint device' signals a piece of machinery, probably something involving a trapdoor and a rotating and lowering table. Both Prospero and Shakespeare are in the business of manufacturing illusion and spectacle, with a premium placed on imposing the suspension of disbelief.

Seeing Shakespeare in Prospero certainly has a seductive quality about it, providing a satisfying vision of completeness, a final meeting with the man himself before mortality draws him away. But in more stern analysis, the Shakespeare–Prospero parallel is perhaps more to do with romance than reality. Certainly, given that the theatre was Shakespeare's life's work, it is inevitable that he drew upon it self-consciously for source material and for self-reflexive observation. But that is probably more to do with convention than self-revelation. The audience-addressing Epilogue in *The Tempest* was more a theatrical standard in Shakespeare's day and is present in other Shakespeare plays, such as *A Midsummer Night's Dream*. Furthermore, seeing Shakespeare as Prospero involves flicking a switch of recognition at choice moments, and therefore ignoring the full range of complexities in Prospero's character.

Prospero is, seen through modern eyes at least, an ambiguous character morally. He is godlike in power, but what sort of god is he? We have seen the problematic dynamic between him and Caliban, and he is also exposed in his relationship with Ariel, his obliging sprite. Ariel is an eager servant, albeit one driven principally by his desire to secure his release. Unlike Caliban, who is a slave in every sense of the word, Ariel is in effect in debt bondage, serving his master until his moral arrears are paid. As we have already seen, the terms of his labour are causing tension between master and servant. The relationship between the two treads a murky ground between affection and coercion. Prospero, for example, swings between referring to Ariel as a 'fine spirit' (I. ii. 420) and as a 'malignant thing' (I. ii. 257). We note that, despite his own magical capabilities, Prospero relies heavily on Ariel for the execution of his plans, and that the animus towards Ariel emerges perhaps most forcefully when Prospero becomes most nervous that his power is contingent on this other. Prospero's management of Ariel, therefore, is of the carrot-and-stick variety, the temptation of eventual freedom backed by direct threats of confinement and violence. But eventually Prospero has to recognize the justice of Ariel's case and release him:

> My Ariel, chick,
> That is thy charge: then to the elements
> Be free, and fare thou well!

V. i. 316–318

It is notable that, while Prospero infuses this liberation with a certain affection, a suggestion of intimacy in the words 'My Ariel, chick', Shakespeare does not give Ariel any final words here – he just disappears with the end of the scene. It perhaps suggests that Ariel was always straining at the leash, serving not through bonds of fidelity but rather through compulsion.

While it is both reductionist and romantic to see Shakespeare in Prospero, the character is certainly more centrally controlling than many others. Iago in *Othello* closely manages the course of events, but does so more through the manipulation of other characters' emotions and desires. Prospero, by contrast, governs the unfolding drama directly, stretching from control of the elements through to the power to command sleep and spirits. Thus the subplots of *The Tempest* cannot escape the shadow of his control; Prospero is always somewhere in the background, figuratively or literally. To some degree, Prospero could reflect contemporary theological debates between advocates of free will (such as Thomas Aquinas) and predestination (Calvin), through the model of life as theatre. Through Prospero, Shakespeare the playwright could be asking us a fundamental question: *Are we really in control of our lives?*

THE TEMPEST

DRAMATIS PERSONÆ

ALONSO, *King of Naples.*
SEBASTIAN, *his brother.*
PROSPERO, *the right Duke of Milan.*
ANTONIO, *his brother, the usurping Duke of Milan.*
FERDINAND, *son to the King of Naples.*
GONZALO, *an honest old Counsellor.*
ADRIAN, } *Lords.*
FRANCISCO, }
CALIBAN, *a savage and deformed Slave.*
TRINCULO, *a Jester.*
STEPHANO, *a drunken Butler.*
MASTER OF A SHIP.
BOATSWAIN.
MARINERS.
MIRANDA, *daughter to Prospero.*
ARIEL, *an airy Spirit.*
IRIS,
CERES,
JUNO, *presented by Spirits.*
NYMPHS,
REAPERS,
OTHER SPIRITS ATTENDING ON PROSPERO.

Magnificoes of Venice, Officers of the Court of Justice, Gaoler,
Servants to Portia, and other Attendants.

SCENE: *Partly at Venice, and partly at Belmont, the seat of Portia,
on the Continent.*

34

THE TEMPEST

ACT FIRST
SCENE I

*On a ship at sea: a tempestuous noise of thunder and
lightning heard.*

Enter a Ship-Master and a Boatswain.

Mast. Boatswain!

Boats. Here, master: what cheer?

Mast. Good, speak to the mariners: fall to 't,
yarely, or we run ourselves aground: bestir,
bestir.   [*Exit.*

Enter Mariners.

Boats. Heigh, my hearts! cheerly, cheerly, my
hearts! yare, yare! Take in the topsail. Tend
to the master's whistle. Blow, till thou burst
thy wind, if room enough!

*Enter Alonso, Sebastian, Antonio, Ferdmand, Gonzalo,
and others.*

Alon. Good boatswain, have care. Where's the   10
master? Play the men.

Boats. I pray now, keep below.

Ant. Where is the master, boatswain?

Boats. Do you not hear him? You mar our labour:
keep your cabins: you do assist the storm.

Gon. Nay, good, be patient.

Boats. When the sea is. Hence! What cares

these roarers for the name of king? To
cabin: silence! trouble us not.

Gon. Good, yet remember whom thou hast   20
     aboard.

Boats. None that I more love than myself. You
     are a counsellor; if you can command these
     elements to silence, and work the peace of the
     present, we will not hand a rope more; use your
     authority: if you cannot, give thanks you have
     lived so long, and make yourself ready in your
     cabin for the mischance of the hour, if it so hap.
     Cheerly, good hearts! Out of our way, I say.   [*Exit.*

Gon. I have great comfort from this fellow: 30
     methinks he hath no drowning mark upon him;
     his complexion is perfect gallows. Stand fast,
     good Fate, to his hanging: make the rope of
     his destiny our cable, for our own doth little
     advantage. If he be not born to be hanged, our
     case is miserable.   [*Exeunt.*

Re-enter Boatswain.

Boats. Down with the topmast! yare! lower, lower!
     Bring her to try with main-course. [*A cry
     within*] A plague upon this howling! they
     are louder than the weather or our office.   40

Re-enter Sebastian, Antonio, and Gonzalo.

     Yet again! what do you here? Shall we give
     o'er, and drown? Have you a mind to sink?

Seb. A pox o' your throat, you bawling, blasphemous,
     incharitable dog!

Boats. Work you, then.

Ant. Hang, cur! hang, you whoreson, insolent noise-
     maker. We are less afraid to be drowned than
     thou art.

Gon. I'll warrant him for drowning; though the

ship were no stronger than a nutshell, and as 50
leaky as an unstanched wench.

Boats. Lay her a-hold, a-hold! set her two courses;
off to sea again; lay her off.

Enter Mariners, wet.

Mariners. All lost! to prayers, to prayers! all lost!

Boats. What, must our mouths be cold?

Gon. The king and prince at prayers! let's assist them,
For our case is as theirs.

Seb.   I'm out of patience.

Ant. We are merely cheated of our lives by drunkards:
This wide-chapp'd rascal,—would thou mightst
                    lie drowning
The washing of ten tides!

Gon.   He'll be hang'd yet, 60
Though every drop of water swear against it,
And gape at widest to glut him.
[*A confused noise within*: 'Mercy on us!'—'We
split, we split!'—'Farewell my wife and children!'—
'Farewell, brother!'—'We split, we split, we split!']

Ant. Let's all sink with the king.

Seb. Let's take leave of him.   [*Exeunt Ant. and Seb.*

Gon. Now would I give a thousand furlongs of sea for
an acre of barren ground, long heath, brown
furze, any thing. The wills above be done! but
I would fain die a dry death.   [*Exeunt.*

SCENE II

The island. Before Prospero's cell.

Enter Prospero and Miranda.

Mir. If by your art, my dearest father, you have
Put the wild waters in this roar, allay them.
The sky, it seems, would pour down stinking pitch,
But that the sea, mounting to the welkin's cheek,
Dashes the fire out. O, I have suffered
With those that I saw suffer! a brave vessel,
Who had, no doubt, some noble creature in her,
Dash'd all to pieces. O, the cry did knock
Against my very heart! Poor souls, they perished!
Had I been any god of power, I would   10
Have sunk the sea within the earth, or ere
It should the good ship so have swallow'd and
The fraughting souls within her.

Pros.   Be collected:
No more amazement: tell your piteous heart
There's no harm done.

Mir.   O, woe the day!

Pros.   No harm.
I have done nothing but in care of thee,
Of thee, my dear one, thee, my daughter, who
Art ignorant of what thou art, nought knowing
Of whence I am, nor that I am more better
Than Prospero, master of a full poor cell,   20
And thy no greater father.

Mir.   More to know
Did never meddle with my thoughts.

Pros.   'Tis time
I should inform thee farther. Lend thy hand,
And pluck my magic garment from me.—So:

> *[Lays down his mantle.*

Lie there, my art. Wipe thou thine eyes; have
   comfort.
The direful spectacle of the wreck, which touch'd
The very virtue of compassion in thee,
I have with such provision in mine art
So safely ordered, that there is no soul,
No, not so much perdition as an hair   30
Betid to any creature in the vessel
Which thou heard'st cry, which thou saw'st sink.
   Sit down;
For thou must now know farther.

Mir.   You have often
Begun to tell me what I am; but stopp'd,
And left me to a bootless inquisition,
Concluding 'Stay: not yet.'

Pros.   The hour's now come;
The very minute bids thee ope thine ear;
Obey, and be attentive. Canst thou remember
A time before we came unto this cell?
I do not think thou canst, for then thou wast not 40
Out three years old.

Mir.   Certainly, sir, I can.

Pros. By what? by any other house or person?
Of any thing the image tell me, that
Hath kept with thy remembrance.

Mir.   'Tis far off,
And rather like a dream than an assurance
That my remembrance warrants. Had I not
Four or five women once that tended me?

Pros. Thou hadst, and more, Miranda. But how is it
That this lives in thy mind? What seest thou else
In the dark backward and abysm of time?   50
If thou remember'st aught ere thou camest here,
How thou camest here thou mayst.

Mir.   But that I do not.

Pros. Twelve year since, Miranda, twelve year since,
Thy father was the Duke of Milan, and
A prince of power.

Mir.   Sir, are not you my father?

Pros. Thy mother was a piece of virtue, and
She said thou wast my daughter; and thy father
Was Duke of Milan; and his only heir
A princess, no worse issued.

Mir.   O the heavens!
What foul play had we, that we came from thence?   60
Or blessed 't we did?

Pros.   Both, both, my girl:
By foul play, as thou say'st, were we heaved thence;
But blessedly holp hither.

Mir.   O, my heart bleeds
To think o' the teen that I have turn'd you to,
Which is from my remembrance! Please you, farther.

Pros. My brother, and thy uncle, call'd Antonio,—
I pray thee, mark me,—that a brother should
Be so perfidious!—he whom, next thyself,
Of all the world I loved, and to him put
The manage of my state; as at that time   70
Through all the signories it was the first,
And Prospero the prime duke, being so reputed
In dignity, and for the liberal arts
Without a parallel; those being all my study,
The government I cast upon my brother,
And to my state grew stranger, being transported
And rapt in secret studies. Thy false uncle—
Dost thou attend me?

Mir.   Sir, most heedfully.

Pros. Being once perfected how to grant suits,
How to deny them, who to advance, and who   80
To trash for over-topping, new created
The creatures that were mine, I say, or changed 'em,
Or else new form'd 'em; having both the key

Of officer and office, set all hearts i' the state
To what tune pleased his ear; that now he was
The ivy which had hid my princely trunk,
And suck'd my verdure out on 't. Thou attend'st not.

Mir.   O, good sir, I do.

Pros.   I pray thee, mark me.
I, thus neglecting worldly ends, all dedicated
To closeness and the bettering of my mind   90
With that which, but by being so retired,
O'er-prized all popular rate, in my false brother
Awaked an evil nature; and my trust,
Like a good parent, did beget of him
A falsehood in its contrary, as great
As my trust was; which had indeed no limit,
A confidence sans bound. He being thus lorded,
Not only with what my revenue yielded,
But what my power might else exact, like one
Who having into truth, by telling of it,   100
Made such a sinner of his memory,
To credit his own lie, he did believe
He was indeed the duke; out o' the substitution,
And executing the outward face of royalty,
With all prerogative:—hence his ambition growing,—
Dost thou hear?

Mir.   Your tale, sir, would cure deafness.

Pros.   To have no screen between this part he play'd
And him he play'd it for, he needs will be
Absolute Milan. Me, poor man, my library
Was dukedom large enough: of temporal royalties   110
He thinks me now incapable; confederates,
So dry he was for sway, wi' the King of Naples
To give him annual tribute, do him homage,
Subject his coronet to his crown, and bend
The dukedom, yet unbow'd,—alas, poor Milan!—
To most ignoble stooping.

Mir.   O the heavens!

Pros. Mark his condition, and the event; then tell me
If this might be a brother.

Mir.   I should sin
To think but nobly of my grandmother:
Good wombs have borne bad sons.

Pros.   Now the condition. 120
This King of Naples, being an enemy
To me inveterate, hearkens my brother's suit;
Which was, that he, in lieu o' the premises,
Of homage and I know not how much tribute,
Should presently extirpate me and mine
Out of the dukedom, and confer fair Milan,
With all the honours, on my brother: whereon,
A treacherous army levied, one midnight
Fated to the purpose, did Antonio open
The gates of Milan; and, i' the dead of darkness, 130
The ministers for the purpose hurried thence
Me and thy crying self.

Mir.   Alack, for pity!
I, not remembering how I cried out then,
Will cry it o'er again: it is a hint
That wrings mine eyes to 't.

Pros.   Hear a little further,
And then I'll bring thee to the present business
Which now's upon 's; without the which, this story
Were most impertinent.

Mir.   Wherefore did they not
That hour destroy us?

Pros.   Well demanded, wench:
My tale provokes that question. Dear, they durst not, 140
So dear the love my people bore me; nor set
A mark so bloody on the business; but
With colours fairer painted their foul ends.
In few, they hurried us aboard a bark,
Bore us some leagues to sea; where they prepared
A rotten carcass of a butt, not rigg'd,
Nor tackle, sail, nor mast; the very rats

Instinctively have quit it: there they hoist us,
To cry to the sea that roared to us; to sigh
To the winds, whose pity, sighing back again,   150
Did us but loving wrong.

Mir.   Alack, what trouble
Was I then to you!

Pros.   O, a cherubin
Thou wast that did preserve me. Thou didst smile,
Infused with a fortitude from heaven,
When I have deck'd the sea with drops full salt,
Under my burthen groan'd; which raised in me
An undergoing stomach, to bear up
Against what should ensue.

Mir.   How came we ashore?

Pros. By Providence divine.
Some food we had, and some fresh water, that   160
A noble Neapolitan, Gonzalo,
Out of his charity, who being then appointed
Master of this design, did give us, with
Rich garments, linens, stuffs and necessaries,
Which since have steaded much; so, of his gentleness,
Knowing I loved my books, he furnish'd me
From mine own library with volumes that
I prize above my dukedom.

Mir.   Would I might
But ever see that man!

Pros.   Now I arise: *[Resumes his mantle.*
Sit still, and hear the last of our sea-sorrow.   170
Here in this island we arrived; and here
Have I, thy schoolmaster, made thee more profit
Than other princess' can, that have more time
For vainer hours, and tutors not so careful.

Mir. Heavens thank you for 't! And now, I pray you, sir,
For still 'tis beating in my mind, your reason
For raising this sea-storm?

Pros.   Know thus far forth.

By accident most strange, bountiful Fortune,
Now my dear lady, hath mine enemies
Brought to this shore; and by my prescience   180
I find my zenith doth depend upon
A most auspicious star, whose influence
If now I court not, but omit, my fortunes
Will ever after droop. Here cease more questions:
Thou art inclined to sleep; 'tis a good dulness.
And give it way: I know thou canst not choose.

            [*Miranda sleeps.*

Come away, servant, come. I am ready now.
Approach, my Ariel, come.

Enter Ariel.

Ari. All hail, great master! grave sir, hail! I come
To answer thy best pleasure; be 't to fly,   190
To swim, to dive into the fire, to ride
On the curl'd clouds, to thy strong bidding task
Ariel and all his quality.

Pros.   Hast thou, spirit,
Perform'd to point the tempest that I bade thee?

Ari. To every article.
I boarded the king's ship; now on the beak,
Now in the waist, the deck, in every cabin,
I flamed amazement: sometime I'ld divide,
And burn in many places; on the topmast,
The yards and bowsprit, would I flame distinctly,   200
Then meet and join. Jove's lightnings, the precursors
O' the dreadful thunder-claps, more momentary
And sight-outrunning were not: the fire and cracks
Of sulphurous roaring the most mighty Neptune
Seem to besiege, and make his bold waves tremble,
Yea, his dread trident shake.

Pros.   My brave spirit!
Who was so firm, so constant, that this coil
Would not infect his reason?

Ari.   Not a soul
But felt a fever of the mad, and play'd

Some tricks of desperation. All but mariners   210
Plunged in the foaming brine, and quit the vessel,
Then all afire with me: the king's son, Ferdinand,
With hair up-staring,—then like reeds, not hair,—
Was the first man that leap'd; cried, 'Hell is empty,
And all the devils are here.'

Pros.   Why, that's my spirit!
But was not this nigh shore?

Ari.   Close by, my master.

Pros. But are they, Ariel, safe?

Ari.   Not a hair perish'd;
On their sustaining garments not a blemish,
But fresher than before: and, as thou badest me,
In troops I have dispersed them 'bout the isle.   220
The king's son have I landed by himself;
Whom I left cooling of the air with sighs
In an odd angle of the isle, and sitting,
His arms in this sad knot.

Pros.   Of the king's ship,
The mariners, say how thou hast disposed,
And all the rest o' the fleet.

Ari.   Safely in harbour
Is the king's ship; in the deep nook, where once
Thou call'dst me up at midnight to fetch dew
From the still-vex'd Bermoothes, there she's hid:
The mariners all under hatches stow'd;   230
Who, with a charm join'd to their suffer'd labour,
I have left asleep: and for the rest o' the fleet,
Which I dispersed, they all have met again,
And are upon the Mediterranean flote,
Bound sadly home for Naples;
Supposing that they saw the king's ship wreck'd,
And his great person perish.

Pros.   Ariel, thy charge
Exactly is perform'd: but there's more work.
What is the time o' the day?

45

Ari.   Past the mid season.

Pros. At least two glasses. The time 'twixt six and now   240
      Must by us both be spent most preciously.

Ari. Is there more toil? Since thou dost give me pains,
      Let me remember thee what thou hast promised,
      Which is not yet perform'd me.

Pros.   How now? moody?
      What is 't thou canst demand?

Ari.   My liberty.

Pros. Before the time be out? no more!

Ari.   I prithee,
      Remember I have done thee worthy service;
      Told thee no lies, made thee no mistakings, served
      Without or grudge or grumblings: thou didst promise
      To bate me a full year.

Pros.   Dost thou forget   250
      From what a torment I did free thee?

Ari.   No.

Pros. Thou dost, and think'st it much to tread the ooze
      Of the salt deep,
      To run upon the sharp wind of the north,
      To do me business in the veins o' the earth
      When it is baked with frost.

Ari.   I do not, sir.

Pros. Thou liest, malignant thing! Hast thou forgot
      The foul witch Sycorax, who with age and envy
      Was grown into a hoop? hast thou forgot her?

Ari. No, sir.

Pros.   Thou hast. Where was she born? speak; tell me.   260

Ari. Sir, in Argier.

Pros.   O, was she so? I must
      Once in a month recount what thou hast been,

Which thou forget'st. This damn'd witch Sycorax,
For mischiefs manifold, and sorceries terrible
To enter human hearing, from Argier,
Thou know'st, was banish'd: for one thing she did
They would not take her life. Is not this true?

Ari. Ay, sir.

Pros. This blue-eyed hag was hither brought with child,
And here was left by the sailors. Thou, my slave, 270
As thou report'st thyself, wast then her servant;
And, for thou wast a spirit too delicate
To act her earthy and abhorr'd commands,
Refusing her grand hests, she did confine thee,
By help of her more potent ministers,
And in her most unmitigable rage,
Into a cloven pine; within which rift
Imprisoned thou didst painfully remain
A dozen years; within which space she died,
And left thee there; where thou didst vent thy
     groans 280
As fast as mill-wheels strike. Then was this island—
Save for the son that she did litter here,
A freckled whelp hag-born—not honour'd with
A human shape.

Ari.   Yes, Caliban her son.

Pros. Dull thing, I say so; he, that Caliban,
Whom now I keep in service. Thou best know'st
What torment I did find thee in; thy groans
Did make wolves howl, and penetrate the breasts
Of ever-angry bears: it was a torment
To lay upon the damn'd, which Sycorax 290
Could not again undo: it was mine art,
When I arrived and heard thee, that made gape
The pine, and let thee out.

Ari.   I thank thee, master.

Pros. If thou more murmur'st, I will rend an oak,
And peg thee in his knotty entrails, till
Thou hast howl'd away twelve winters.

Ari.   Pardon, master:
    I will be correspondent to command,
    And do my spiriting gently.

Pros.   Do so; and after two days
    1 will discharge thee.

Ari.   That's my noble master!
    What shall I do? say what; what shall I do?   300

Pros.   Go make thyself like a nymph o' the sea: be subject
    To no sight but thine and mine; invisible
    To every eyeball else. Go take this shape.
    And hither come in 't: go, hence with diligence!
                        [Exit Ariel.
    Awake, dear heart, awake! thou hast slept well;
    Awake!

Mir.   The strangeness of your story put
    Heaviness in me.

Pros.   Shake it off. Come on;
    We'll visit Caliban my slave, who never
    Yields us kind answer.

Mir.   'Tis a villain, sir,
    I do not love to look on.

Pros.   But, as 'tis,   310
    We cannot miss him: he does make our fire,
    Fetch in our wood, and serves in offices
    That profit us. What, ho! slave! Caliban!
    Thou earth, thou! speak.

Cal.   [*Within*] There's wood enough within.

Pros.   Come forth, I say! there's other business for thee:
    Come, thou tortoise! when?

Re-enter Ariel like a water-nymph.

    Fine apparition! My quaint Ariel,
    Hark in thine ear.

Ari.   My lord, it shall be done.   [*Exit.*

Pros.   Thou poisonous slave, got by the devil himself
      Upon thy wicked dam, come forth!   320

Enter Caliban.

Cal.   As wicked dew as e'er my mother brush'd
      With raven's feather from unwholesome fen
      Drop on you both! a south-west blow on ye
      And blister you all o'er!

Pros.   For this, be sure, to-night thou shalt have cramps,
      Side-stitches that shall pen thy breath up; urchins
      Shall, for that vast of night that they may work,
      All exercise on thee; thou shalt be pinch'd
      As thick as honeycomb, each pinch more stinging
      Than bees that made 'em.

Cal.   I must eat my dinner.   330
      This island's mine, by Sycorax my mother,
      Which thou takest from me. When thou camest first,
      Thou strokedst me, and madest much of me;
                 wouldst give me
      Water with berries in 't; and teach me how
      To name the bigger light, and how the less,
      That burn by day and night: and then I loved thee,
      And show'd thee all the qualities o' th' isle,
      The fresh springs, brine-pits, barren place and fertile:
      Cursed be I that did so! All the charms
      Of Sycorax, toads, beetles, bats, light on you!   340
      For I am all the subjects that you have,
      Which first was mine own king: and here you sty me
      In this hard rock, whiles you do keep from me
      The rest o' th' island.

Pros.   Thou most lying slave,
      Whom stripes may move, not kindness! I have used thee,
      Filth as thou art, with human care; and lodged thee
      In mine own cell, till thou didst seek to violate
      The honour of my child.

Cal.   O ho, O ho! would 't had been done!
      Thou didst prevent me; I had peopled else   350
      This isle with Calibans.

Pros.   Abhorred slave,
Which any print of goodness wilt not take,
Being capable of all ill! I pitied thee,
Took pains to make thee speak, taught thee each hour
One thing or other: when thou didst not, savage,
Know thine own meaning, but wouldst gabble like
A thing most brutish, I endow'd thy purposes
With words that made them known. But thy vile race,
Though thou didst learn, had that in 't which good natures
Could not abide to be with; therefore wast thou   360
Deservedly confined into this rock,
Who hadst deserved more than a prison.

Cal.   You taught me language; and my profit on 't
Is, I know how to curse. The red plague rid you
For learning me your language!

Pros.   Hag-seed, hence!
Fetch us in fuel; and be quick, thou 'rt best,
To answer other business. Shrug'st thou, malice?
If thou neglect'st, or dost unwillingly
What I command, I'll rack thee with old cramps,
Fill all thy bones with aches, make thee roar,   370
That beasts shall tremble at thy din.

Cal.   No, pray thee.
[*Aside*] I must obey: his art is of such power,
It would control my dam's god, Setebos,
And make a vassal of him.

Pros.   So, slave; hence!   [*Exit Caliban.*

Re-enter Ariel, invisible, playing and singing; Ferdinand following.

ARIEL'S SONG

Come unto these yellow sands,
And then take hands:
Courtsied when you have and kiss'd
The wild waves whist:
Foot it featly here and there;   380
And, sweet sprites, the burthen bear.
Hark, hark!
Burthen [*dispersedly*]. Bow-wow.

Ari. The watch dogs bark:
Burthen [*dispersedly*]. Bow-wow.
    Ari. Hark, hark! I hear
The strain of strutting chanticleer
    Cry, Cock-a-diddle-dow.

Fer.   Where should this music be? i' th' air or th' earth?
It sounds no more: and, sure, it waits upon
Some god o' th' island. Sitting on a bank,
Weeping again the king my father's wreck,   390
This music crept by me upon the waters,
Allaying both their fury and my passion
With its sweet air: thence I have follow'd it,
Or it hath drawn me rather. But 'tis gone.
No, it begins again.

Ariel sings.

Full fathom five thy father lies;
  Of his bones are coral made;
Those are pearls that were his eyes:
  Nothing of him that doth fade,
But doth suffer a sea-change   400
Into something rich and strange.
Sea-nymphs hourly ring his knell:
        Burthen: Ding-dong.

Ari.   Hark! now I hear them,—Ding-dong, bell.

Fer.   The ditty does remember my drown'd father.
This is no mortal business, nor no sound
That the earth owes:—I hear it now above me.

Pros.   The fringed curtains of thine eye advance,
And say what thou seest yond.

Mir.   What is 't? a spirit?
Lord, how it looks about! Believe me, sir,   410
It carries a brave form. But 'tis a spirit.

Pros.   No, wench; it eats and sleeps and hath such senses
As we have, such. This gallant which thou seest
Was in the wreck; and, but he's something stain'd
With grief, that's beauty's canker, thou mightst call him

A goodly person: he hath lost his fellows,
And strays about to find 'em.

Mir.   I might call him
A thing divine; for nothing natural
I ever saw so noble.

Pros.   [*Aside*] It goes on, I see,
As my soul prompts it. Spirit, fine spirit! I'll free thee   420
Within two days for this.

Fer.   Most sure, the goddess
On whom these airs attend! Vouchsafe my prayer
May know if you remain upon this island;
And that you will some good instruction give
How I may bear me here: my prime request,
Which I do last pronounce, is, O you wonder!
If you be maid or no?

Mir.   No wonder, sir;
But certainly a maid.

Fer.   My language! heavens!
I am the best of them that speak this speech,
Were I but where 'tis spoken.

Pros.   How? the best?   430
What wert thou, if the King of Naples heard thee?

Fer. A single thing, as I am now, that wonders
To hear thee speak of Naples. He does hear me;
And that he does I weep: myself am Naples,
Who with mine eyes, never since at ebb, beheld
The king my father wreck'd.

Mir.   Alack, for mercy!

Fer. Yes, faith, and all his lords; the Duke of Milan
And his brave son being twain.

Pros.   [*Aside*] The Duke of Milan
And his more braver daughter could control thee,
If now 'twere fit to do 't. At the first sight   440
They have changed eyes. Delicate Ariel,

	I'll set thee free for this. [*To Fer.*] A word, good sir;
	I fear you have done yourself some wrong: a word.
Mir.	Why speaks my father so ungently? This
	Is the third man that e'er I saw; the first
	That e'er I sigh'd for: pity move my father
	To be inclined my way!
Fer.	O, if a virgin,
	And your affection not gone forth, I'll make you
	The queen of Naples.
Pros.	Soft, sir! one word more.
	[*Aside*] They are both in either's powers: but this
	swift business
	I must uneasy make, lest too light winning
	Make the prize light. [*To Fer.*] One word
	more; I charge thee
	That thou attend me: thou dost here usurp
	The name thou owest not; and hast put thyself
	Upon this island as a spy, to win it
	From me, the lord on 't.
Fer.	No, as I am a man.
Mir.	There's nothing ill can dwell in such a temple:
	If the ill spirit have so fair a house,
	Good things will strive to dwell with 't.
Pros.	Follow me.
	Speak not you for him; he's a traitor. Come;
	I'll manacle thy neck and feet together:
	Sea-water shalt thou drink; thy food shall be
	The fresh-brook muscles, wither'd roots, and husks
	Wherein the acorn cradled. Follow.
Fer.	No;
	I will resist such entertainment till
	Mine enemy has more power.
	[*Draws, and is charmed from moving.*
Mir.	O dear father,
	Make not too rash a trial of him, for
	He's gentle, and not fearful.

450

460

Pros.   What! I say,
My foot my tutor? Put thy sword up, traitor;
Who makest a show, but darest not strike, thy conscience   470
Is so possess'd with guilt: come from thy ward;
For I can here disarm thee with this stick
And make thy weapon drop.

Mir.   Beseech you, father.

Pros. Hence! hang not on my garments.

Mir.   Sir, have pity;
I'll be his surety.

Pros.   Silence! one word more
Shall make me chide thee, if not hate thee. What!
An advocate for an impostor! hush!
Thou think'st there is no more such shapes as he,
Having seen but him and Caliban: foolish wench!
To the most of men this is a Caliban,   480
And they to him are angels.

Mir.   My affections
Are, then, most humble; I have no ambition
To see a goodlier man.

Pros.   Come on; obey;
Thy nerves are in their infancy again,
And have no vigour in them.

Fer.   So they are:
My spirits, as in a dream, are all bound up.
My father's loss, the weakness which I feel,
The wreck of all my friends, nor this man's threats,
To whom I am subdued, are but light to me,
Might I but through my prison once a day   490
Behold this maid: all comers else o' th' earth
Let liberty make use of; space enough
Have I in such a prison.

Pros.   [*Aside*] It works. [*To Ari.*] Come on.
Thou hast done well, fine Ariel! [*To Fer.*]
                Follow me.
[*To Ari.*] Hark what thou else shalt do me.

Mir.   Be of comfort;
My father's of a better nature, sir,
Than he appears by speech: this is unwonted
Which now came from him.

Pros.   Thou shalt be as free
As mountain winds: but then exactly do
All points of my command.

Ari.   To the syllable.   500

Pros. Come, follow. Speak not for him.   [*Exeunt.*

ACT SECOND
SCENE I

Another part of the island.

*Enter Alonso, Sebastian, Antonio, Gonzalo,
Adrian, Francisco, and others.*

Gon. Beseech you, sir, be merry; you have cause,
So have we all, of joy, for our escape
Is much beyond our loss. Our hint of woe
Is common; every day, some sailor's wife,
The masters of some merchant, and the merchant,
Have just our theme of woe; but for the miracle,
I mean our preservation, few in millions
Can speak like us: then wisely, good sir, weigh
Our sorrow with our comfort.

Alon.   Prithee, peace.

Seb. He receives comfort like cold porridge.   10

Ant. The visitor will not give him o'er so.

Seb. Look, he's winding up the watch of his wit; by
and by it will strike.

55

Gon.   Sir,—

Seb.   One: tell.

Gon.   When every grief is entertained that's offer'd,
Comes to the entertainer—

Seb.   A dollar.

Gon.   Dolour comes to him, indeed: you have spoken
truer than you purposed.   20

Seb.   You have taken it wiselier than I meant you
should.

Gon.   Therefore, my lord,—

Ant.   Fie, what a spendthrift is he of his tongue!

Alon.   I prithee, spare.

Gon.   Well, I have done: but yet,—

Seb.   He will be talking.

Ant.   Which, of he or Adrian, for a good wager,
first begins to crow?

Seb.   The old cock.   30

Ant.   The cockerel.

Seb.   Done. The wager?

Ant.   A laughter.

Seb.   A match!

Adr.   Though this island seem to be desert,—

Seb.   Ha, ha, ha!—So, you 're paid.

Adr.   Uninhabitable and almost inaccessible,—

Seb.   Yet,—

Adr.   Yet,—

Ant.   He could not miss 't.   40

Adr.   It must needs be of subtle, tender and delicate
temperance.

Ant.   Temperance was a delicate wench.

Seb.   Ay, and a subtle; as he most learnedly
delivered.

Adr.   The air breathes upon us here most sweetly.

Seb.   As if it had lungs, and rotten ones.

Ant.   Or as 'twere perfumed by a fen.

Gon.   Here is everything advantageous to life.

Ant.   True; save means to live.   50

Seb.   Of that there's none, or little.

Gon.   How lush and lusty the grass looks! how
green!

Ant.   The ground, indeed, is tawny.

Seb.   With an eye of green in 't.

Ant.   He misses not much.

Seb.   No; he doth but mistake the truth totally.

Gon.   But the rarity of it is,—which is indeed almost
beyond credit,—

Seb.   As many vouched rarities are.   60

Gon.   That our garments, being, as they were,
drenched in the sea, hold, notwithstanding, their
freshness and glosses, being rather new-dyed
than stained with salt water.

Ant.   If but one of his pockets could speak, would
it not say he lies?

Seb.   Ay, or very falsely pocket up his report.

Gon.   Methinks our garments are now as fresh as
when we put them on first in Afric, at the

marriage of the king's fair daughter Claribel to 70
the King of Tunis.

Seb. 'Twas a sweet marriage, and we prosper well
in our return.

Adr. Tunis was never graced before with such a
paragon to their queen.

Gon. Not since widow Dido's time.

Ant. Widow! a pox o' that! How came that
widow in? widow Dido!

Seb. What if he had said 'widower Æneas' too?
Good Lord, how you take it! 80

Adr. 'Widow Dido' said you? you make me study
of that: she was of Carthage, not of Tunis.

Gon. This Tunis, sir, was Carthage.

Adr. Carthage?

Gon. I assure you, Carthage.

Ant. His word is more than the miraculous harp.

Seb. He hath raised the wall, and houses too.

Ant. What impossible matter will he make easy
next?

Seb. I think he will carry this island home in his 90
pocket, and give it his son for an apple.

Ant. And, sowing the kernels of it in the sea, bring
forth more islands.

Gon. Ay.

Ant. Why, in good time.

Gon. Sir, we were talking that our garments seem
now as fresh as when we were at Tunis at the
marriage of your daughter, who is now queen.

Ant. And the rarest that e'er came there.

Seb.	Bate, I beseech you, widow Dido.	100

Ant. O widow Dido! ay, widow Dido.

Gon. Is not, sir, my doublet as fresh as the first day
I wore it? I mean, in a sort.

Ant. That sort was well fished for.

Gon. When I wore it at your daughter's marriage?

Alon. You cram these words into mine ears against
The stomach of my sense. Would I had never
Married my daughter there! For, coming thence,
My son is lost, and, in my rate, she too,
Who is so far from Italy removed   110
I ne'er again shall see her. O thou mine heir
Of Naples and of Milan, what strange fish
Hath made his meal on thee?

Fran.   Sir, he may live:
I saw him beat the surges under him,
And ride upon their backs; he trod the water,
Whose enmity he flung aside, and breasted
The surge most swoln that met him; his bold head
'Bove the contentious waves he kept, and oar'd
Himself with his good arms in lusty stroke
To the shore, that o'er his wave-worn basis bow'd,   120
As stooping to relieve him: I not doubt
He came alive to land.

Alon.   No, no, he's gone.

Seb. Sir, you may thank yourself for this great loss,
That would not bless our Europe with your daughter,
But rather lose her to an African;
Where she, at least, is banish'd from your eye,
Who hath cause to wet the grief on 't.

Alon.   Prithee, peace.

Seb. You were kneel'd to, and importuned otherwise,
By all of us; and the fair soul herself
Weigh'd between loathness and obedience, at   130
Which end o' the beam should bow. We have
       lost your son,

59

I fear, for ever: Milan and Naples have
Mo widows in them of this business' making
Than we bring men to comfort them:
The fault's your own.

Alon.   So is the dear'st o' the loss.

Gon. My lord Sebastian,
The truth you speak doth lack some gentleness,
And time to speak it in: you rub the sore,
When you should bring the plaster.

Seb.   Very well.

Ant. And most chirurgeonly.   140

Gon. It is foul weather in us all, good sir,
When you are cloudy.

Seb.   Foul weather?

Ant.   Very foul.

Gon. Had I plantation of this isle, my lord,—

Ant. He'ld sow 't with nettle-seed.

Seb.   Or docks, or mallows.

Gon. And were the king on 't, what would I do?

Seb. 'Scape being drunk for want of wine.

Gon. I' the commonwealth I would by contraries
Execute all things; for no kind of traffic
Would I admit; no name of magistrate;
Letters should not be known; riches, poverty,   150
And use of service, none; contract, succession,
Bourn, bound of land, tilth, vineyard, none;
No use of metal, corn, or wine, or oil;
No occupation; all men idle, all;
And women too, but innocent and pure;
No sovereignty;—

Seb.   Yet he would be king on 't.

Ant. The latter end of his commonwealth forgets
the beginning.

Gon. All things in common nature should produce
Without sweat or endeavour: treason, felony,   160
Sword, pike, knife, gun, or need of any engine,
Would I not have; but nature should bring forth,
Of it own kind, all foison, all abundance,
To feed my innocent people.

Seb. No marrying 'mong his subjects?

Ant. None, man; all idle; whores and knaves.

Gon. I would with such perfection govern, sir,
To excel the golden age.

Seb.   'Save his majesty!

Ant. Long live Gonzalo!

Gon.   And,—do you mark me, sir?

Alon. Prithee, no more: thou dost talk nothing to   170
me.

Gon. I do well believe your highness; and did it to
minister occasion to these gentlemen, who are
of such sensible and nimble lungs that they
always use to laugh at nothing.

Ant. 'Twas you we laughed at.

Gon. Who in this kind of merry fooling am nothing
to you: so you may continue, and laugh at
nothing still.

Ant. What a blow was there given!   180

Seb. An it had not fallen flat-long.

Gon. You are gentlemen of brave mettle; you would
lift the moon out of her sphere, if she would
continue in it five weeks without changing.

Enter Ariel (invisible) playing solemn music.

61

Seb.   We would so, and then go a bat-fowling.

Ant.   Nay, good my lord, be not angry.

Gon.   No, I warrant you; I will not adventure
my discretion so weakly. Will you laugh
me asleep, for I am very heavy?

Ant.   Go sleep, and hear us.   190

             [*All sleep except Alon., Seb., and Ant.*

Alon.   What, all so soon asleep! I wish mine eyes
Would, with themselves, shut up my thoughts: I find
They are inclined to do so.

Seb.   Please you, sir,
Do not omit the heavy offer of it:
It seldom visits sorrow; when it doth,
It is a comforter.

Ant.   We two, my lord,
Will guard your person while you take your rest,
And watch your safety.

Alon.   Thank you.—Wondrous heavy.

             [*Alonso sleeps. Exit Ariel.*

Seb.   What a strange drowsiness possesses them!

Ant.   It is the quality o' the climate.

Seb.   Why   200
Doth it not then our eyelids sink? I find not
Myself disposed to sleep.

Ant.   Nor I; my spirits are nimble.
They fell together all, as by consent;
They dropp'd, as by a thunder-stroke. What might,
Worthy Sebastian?—O, what might?—No more:—
And yet methinks I see it in thy face,
What thou shouldst be: the occasion speaks thee; and
My strong imagination sees a crown
Dropping upon thy head.

Seb.   What, art thou waking?

Ant.   Do you not hear me speak?

Seb.   I do; and surely   210
It is a sleepy language, and thou speak'st
Out of thy sleep. What is it thou didst say?
This is a strange repose, to be asleep
With eyes wide open; standing, speaking, moving,
And yet so fast asleep.

Ant.   Noble Sebastian,
Thou let'st thy fortune sleep—die, rather; wink'st
Whiles thou art waking.

Seb.   Thou dost snore distinctly;
There's meaning in thy snores.

Ant.   I am more serious than my custom: you
Must be so too, if heed me; which to do   220
Trebles thee o'er.

Seb.   Well, I am standing water.

Ant.   I'll teach you how to flow.

Seb.   Do so: to ebb
Hereditary sloth instructs me.

Ant.   O,
If you but knew how you the purpose cherish
Whiles thus you mock it! how, in stripping it,
You more invest it! Ebbing men, indeed,
Most often do so near the bottom run
By their own fear or sloth.

Seb.   Prithee, say on:
The setting of thine eye and cheek proclaim
A matter from thee; and a birth, indeed,   230
Which throes thee much to yield.

Ant.   Thus, sir:
Although this lord of weak remembrance, this,
Who shall be of as little memory
When he is earth'd, hath here almost persuaded,—
For he's a spirit of persuasion, only
Professes to persuade,—the king his son's alive,

63

'Tis as impossible that he's undrown'd
As he that sleeps here swims.

Seb.   I have no hope
That he's undrown'd.

Ant.   O, out of that 'no hope'
What great hope have you! no hope that way is   240
Another way so high a hope that even
Ambition cannot pierce a wink beyond,
But doubt discovery there. Will you grant with me
That Ferdinand is drown'd?

Seb.   He's gone.

Ant.   Then, tell me.
Who's the next heir of Naples?

Seb.   Claribel.

Ant.   She that is queen of Tunis, she that dwells
Ten leagues beyond man's life; she that from Naples
Can have no note, unless the sun were post,—
The man i' the moon's too slow,—till new-born chins
Be rough and razorable; she that from whom   250
We all were sea-swallow'd, though some cast again,
And by that destiny, to perform an act
Whereof what's past is prologue; what to come,
In yours and my discharge.

Seb.   What stuff is this! how say you?
'Tis true, my brother's daughter's queen of Tunis;
So is she heir of Naples; 'twixt which regions
There is some space.

Ant.   A space whose every cubit
Seems to cry out, 'How shall that Claribel
Measure us back to Naples? Keep in Tunis,
And let Sebastian wake.' Say, this were death   260
That now hath seized them; why, they were no worse
Than now they are. There be that can rule Naples
As well as he that sleeps; lords that can prate
As amply and unnecessarily
As this Gonzalo; I myself could make

A chough of as deep chat. O, that you bore
The mind that I do! what a sleep were this
For your advancement! Do you understand me?

Seb.   Methinks I do.

Ant.   And how does your content
Tender your own good fortune?

Seb.   I remember   270
You did supplant your brother Prospero.

Ant.   True:
And look how well my garments sit upon me;
Much feater than before: my brother's servants
Were then my fellows; now they are my men.

Seb.   But, for your conscience.

Ant.   Ay, sir; where lies that? if 'twere a kibe,
'T would put me to my slipper: but I feel not
This deity in my bosom: twenty consciences,
That stand 'twixt me and Milan, candied be they,
And melt, ere they molest! Here lies your brother,   280
No better than the earth he lies upon,
If he were that which now he's like, that's dead;
Whom I, with this obedient steel, three inches of it,
Can lay to bed for ever; whiles you, doing thus,
To the perpetual wink for aye might put
This ancient morsel, this Sir Prudence, who
Should not upbraid our course. For all the rest,
They'll take suggestion as a cat laps milk;
They'll tell the clock to any business that
We say befits the hour.

Seb.   Thy case, dear friend,   290
Shall be my precedent; as thou got'st Milan,
I'll come by Naples. Draw thy sword: one stroke
Shall free thee from the tribute which thou payest;
And I the king shall love thee.

Ant.   Draw together;
And when I rear my hand, do you the like,
To fall it on Gonzalo.

65

Seb.   O, but one word.   [*They talk apart.*

Re-enter Ariel invisible.

Ari.   My master through his art foresees the danger
          That you, his friend, are in; and sends me forth,—
          For else his project dies,—to keep them living.
                              [*Sings in Gonzalo's ear.*
                    While you here do snoring lie,   300
                    Open-eyed conspiracy
                              His time doth take.
                    If of life you keep a care,
                    Shake off slumber, and beware:
                              Awake, awake!

Ant.   Then let us both be sudden.

Gon.   Now, good angels
          Preserve the king!   [*They wake.*

Alon.   Why, how now? ho, awake!—Why are you drawn?
          Wherefore this ghastly looking?

Gon.   What's the matter?

Seb.   Whiles we stood here securing your repose,   310
          Even now, we heard a hollow burst of bellowing
          Like bulls, or rather lions: did 't not wake you?
          It struck mine ear most terribly.

Alon.   I heard nothing.

Ant.   O, 'twas a din to fright a monster's ear,
          To make an earthquake! sure, it was the roar
          Of a whole herd of lions.

Alon.   Heard you this, Gonzalo?

Gon.   Upon mine honour, sir, I heard a humming,
          And that a strange one too, which did awake me:
          I shaked you, sir, and cried: as mine eyes open'd,
          I saw their weapons drawn:—there was a noise,   320
          That's verily. 'Tis best we stand upon our guard,
          Or that we quit this place: let's draw our weapons.

Alon.	Lead off this ground; and let's make further search For my poor son.
Gon.	Heavens keep him from these beasts! For he is, sure, i' th' island.
Alon.	Lead away.
Ari.	Prospero my lord shall know what I have done: So, king, go safely on to seek thy son. [*Exeunt.*

SCENE II

Another part of the island.

*Enter Caliban with a burden of wood. A noise
of thunder heard.*

Cal. All the infections that the sun sucks up
From bogs, fens, flats, on Prosper fall, and make him
By inch-meal a disease! his spirits hear me,
And yet I needs must curse. But they'll nor pinch,
Fright me with urchin-shows, pitch me i' the mire,
Nor lead me, like a firebrand, in the dark
Out of my way, unless he bid 'em: but
For every trifle are they set upon me;
Sometime like apes, that mow and chatter at me.
And after bite me; then like hedgehogs, which   10
Lie tumbling in my barefoot way, and mount
Their pricks at my footfall; sometime am I
All wound with adders, who with cloven tongues
Do hiss me into madness.

Enter Trinculo.

Lo, now, lo!
Here comes a spirit of his, and to torment me
For bringing wood in slowly. I'll fall flat;
Perchance he will not mind me.

67

Trin. Here's neither bush nor shrub, to bear off
any weather at all, and another storm brewing;
I hear it sing i' the wind: yond same black cloud, 20
yond huge one, looks like a foul bombard that
would shed his liquor. If it should thunder as it
did before, I know not where to hide my head:
yond same cloud cannot choose but fall by pail-
fuls. What have we here? a man or a fish? dead
or alive? A fish: he smells like a fish; a very
ancient and fish-like smell; a kind of not of the
newest Poor-John. A strange fish! Were I in
England now, as once I was, and had but this fish
painted, not a holiday fool there but would give 30
a piece of silver: there would this monster make
a man; any strange beast there makes a man:
when they will not give a doit to relieve a lame
beggar, they will lay out ten to see a dead Indian.
Legged like a man! and his fins like arms! Warm
o' my troth! I do now let loose my opinion; hold
it no longer: this is no fish, but an islander, that
hath lately suffered by a thunderbolt. [*Thunder*]
Alas, the storm is come again! my best way is to
creep under his gaberdine; there is no other shelter 40
hereabout: misery acquaints a man with strange
bed-fellows. I will here shroud till the dregs of
the storm be past.

Enter Stephano, singing: a bottle in his hand.

Ste.   I shall no more to sea, to sea,
              Here shall I die a-shore,—

This is a very scurvy tune to sing at a man's
funeral: well, here's my comfort.   [*Drinks*]
[*Sings*]
The master, the swabber, the boatswain, and I,
        The gunner, and his mate,
Loved Moll, Meg, and Marian, and Margery, 50
        But none of us cared for Kate;
        For she had a tongue with a tang,
        Would cry to a sailor, Go hang!
She loved not the savour of tar nor of pitch;

Yet a tailor might scratch her where'er she did itch.
    Then, to sea, boys, and let her go hang!

This is a scurvy tune too: but here's my comfort. [*Drinks*]

Cal. Do not torment me:—O!

Ste. What's the matter? Have we devils here?
Do you put tricks upon 's with salvages and   60
men of Ind, ha? I have not scaped drowning, to
be afeard now of your four legs; for it hath been
said, As proper a man as ever went on four legs
cannot make him give ground; and it shall be
said so again, while Stephano breathes at nostrils.

Cal. The spirit torments me:—O!

Ste. This is some monster of the isle with
four legs, who hath got, as I take it, an ague.
Where the devil should he learn our language?
I will give him some relief, if it be but for that.   70
If I can recover him, and keep him tame, and get
to Naples with him, he's a present for any
emperor that ever trod on neat's-leather.

Cal. Do not torment me, prithee; I'll bring my
wood home faster.

Ste. He's in his fit now, and does not talk after
the wisest. He shall taste of my bottle: if he
have never drunk wine afore, it will go near to
remove his fit. If I can recover him, and keep
him tame, I will not take too much for him; he   80
shall pay for him that hath him, and that soundly.

Cal. Thou dost me yet but little hurt; thou wilt
anon, I know it by thy trembling: now Prosper
works upon thee.

Ste. Come on your ways; open your mouth; here
is that which will give language to you, cat:
open your mouth; this will shake your shaking,
I can tell you, and that soundly: you cannot tell
who's your friend: open your chaps again.

Trin. I should know that voice: it should be—   90
but he is drowned: and these are devils:—O
defend me!

Ste. Four legs and two voices,—a most delicate
monster! His forward voice, now, is to speak
well of his friend; his backward voice is to utter
foul speeches and to detract. If all the wine in
my bottle will recover him, I will help his ague.
Come:—Amen! I will pour some in thy other
mouth.

Trin. Stephano!   100

Ste. Doth thy other mouth call me? Mercy,
mercy! This is a devil, and no monster: I
will leave him; I have no long spoon.

Trin. Stephano! If thou beest Stephano, touch me,
and speak to me; for I am Trinculo,—be not
afeard,—thy good friend Trinculo.

Ste. If thou beest Trinculo, come forth: I'll pull
thee by the lesser legs: if any be Trinculo's
legs, these are they. Thou art very Trinculo
indeed! How camest thou to be the siege of   110
this moon-calf? can he vent Trinculos?

Trin. I took him to be killed with a thunder-stroke.
But art thou not drowned, Stephano? I hope,
now, thou art not drowned. Is the storm overblown? I hid me under the dead moon-calf's
gaberdine for fear of the storm. And art thou living,
Stephano? O Stephano, two Neapolitans 'scaped!

Ste. Prithee, do not turn me about; my stomach is
not constant.

Cal. [*Aside*] These be fine things, an if they be
        not sprites.   120
That's a brave god, and bears celestial liquor:
I will kneel to him.

Ste. How didst thou 'scape? How camest thou

hither? swear, by this bottle, how thou camest
hither. I escaped upon a butt of sack, which the
sailors heaved o'erboard, by this bottle! which I
made of the bark of a tree with mine own hands,
since I was cast ashore.

Cal.   I'll swear, upon that bottle, to be thy true
      subject; for the liquor is not earthly.   130

Ste.   Here; swear, then, how thou escapedst.

Trin.   Swum ashore, man, like a duck: I can swim
      like a duck, I'll be sworn.

Ste.   Here, kiss the book. Though thou canst swim
      like a duck, thou art made like a goose.

Trin.   O Stephano, hast any more of this?

Ste.   The whole butt, man: my cellar is in a rock by
      the sea-side, where my wine is hid. How now,
      moon-calf! how does thine ague?

Cal.   Hast thou not dropp'd from heaven?   140

Ste.   Out o' the moon, I do assure thee: I was the
      man i' the moon when time was.

Cal.   I have seen thee in her, and I do adore thee: my
      mistress show'd me thee, and thy dog, and thy
      bush.

Ste.   Come, swear to that; kiss the book: I will
      furnish it anon with new contents: swear.

Trin.   By this good light, this is a very shallow
      monster! I afeard of him! A very weak
      monster! The man i' the moon! A most
      poor credulous monster! Well drawn, monster,   150
      in good sooth!

Cal.   I'll show thee every fertile inch o' th' island;
      and I will kiss thy foot: I prithee, be my god.

Trin.   By this light, a most perfidious and drunken
      monster! when 's god's asleep, he'll rob his bottle.

Cal.   I'll kiss thy foot; I'll swear myself thy subject.

Ste.   Come on, then; down, and swear.

Trin.   I shall laugh myself to death at this puppy-
headed monster. A most scurvy monster! I
could find in my heart to beat him,—   160

Ste.   Come, kiss.

Trin.   But that the poor monster's in drink. An
abominable monster!

Cal.   I'll show thee the best springs; I'll pluck thee
    berries;
I'll fish for thee, and get thee wood enough.
A plague upon the tyrant that I serve!
I'll bear him no more sticks, but follow thee,
Thou wondrous man.

Trin.   A most ridiculous monster, to make a wonder
of a poor drunkard!   170

Cal.   I prithee, let me bring thee where crabs grow;
And I with my long nails will dig thee pig-nuts;
Show thee a jay's nest, and instruct thee how
To snare the nimble marmoset; I'll bring thee
To clustering filberts, and sometimes I'll get thee
Young scamels from the rock. Wilt thou go with me?

Ste.   I prithee now, lead the way, without any more
talking. Trinculo, the king and all our company
else being drowned, we will inherit here: here;
bear my bottle: fellow Trinculo, we'll fill him   180
by and by again.

Cal.   [*Sings drunkenly*]
       Farewell, master; farewell, farewell!

Trin.   A howling monster; a drunken monster!

Cal.   No more dams I'll make for fish;
          Nor fetch in firing
          At requiring;
       Nor scrape trencher, nor wash dish:

'Ban, 'Ban, Cacaliban
Has a new master:—get a new man.
Freedom, hey-day! hey-day, freedom! free-   190
dom, hey-day, freedom!

Ste.   O brave monster! Lead the way.   [*Exeunt.*

ACT THIRD
SCENE I

Before Prospero's cell.

Enter Ferdinand, bearing a log.

Fer.   There be some sports are painful, and their labour
Delight in them sets off: some kinds of baseness
Are nobly undergone, and most poor matters
Point to rich ends. This my mean task
Would be as heavy to me as odious, but
The mistress which I serve quickens what's dead,
And makes my labours pleasures: O, she is
Ten times more gentle than her father's crabbed,
And he's composed of harshness. I must remove
Some thousands of these logs, and pile them up,   10
Upon a sore injunction: my sweet mistress
Weeps when she sees me work, and says, such baseness
Had never like executor. I forget:
But these sweet thoughts do even refresh my labours,
Most busy lest, when I do it.

Enter Miranda; and Prospero at a distance, unseen.

Mir.   Alas, now, pray you,
Work not so hard: I would the lightning had
Burnt up those logs that you are enjoin'd to pile!
Pray, set it down, and rest you: when this burns,
'Twill weep for having wearied you. My father
Is hard at study; pray, now, rest yourself;   20
He's safe for these three hours.

Fer.   O most dear mistress,

The sun will set before I shall discharge
What I must strive to do.

Mir.   If you'll sit down,
I'll bear your logs the while: pray, give me that;
I'll carry it to the pile.

Fer.   No, precious creature;
I had rather crack my sinews, break my back,
Than you should such dishonour undergo,
While I sit lazy by.

Mir.   It would become me
As well as it does you: and I should do it
With much more ease; for my good will is to it,   30
And yours it is against.

Pros.   Poor worm, thou art infected!
This visitation shows it.

Mir.   You look wearily.

Fer.   No, noble mistress; 'tis fresh morning with me
When you are by at night. I do beseech you,—
Chiefly that I might set it in my prayers,—
What is your name?

Mir.   Miranda.—O my father,
I have broke your hest to say so!

Fer.   Admired Miranda!
Indeed the top of admiration! worth
What's dearest to the world! Full many a lady
I have eyed with best regard, and many a time   40
The harmony of their tongues hath into bondage
Brought my too diligent ear: for several virtues
Have I liked several women; never any
With so full soul, but some defect in her
Did quarrel with the noblest grace she owed,
And put it to the foil: but you, O you,
So perfect and so peerless, are created
Of every creature's best!

Mir.   I do not know
One of my sex; no woman's face remember,

74

Save, from my glass, mine own; nor have I seen   50
More that I may call men than you, good friend,
And my dear father: how features are abroad,
I am skilless of; but, by my modesty,
The jewel in my dower, I would not wish
Any companion in the world but you;
Nor can imagination form a shape,
Besides yourself, to like of. But I prattle
Something too wildly, and my father's precepts
I therein do forget.

Fer.   I am, in my condition,
A prince, Miranda; I do think, a king;   60
I would, not so!—and would no more endure
This wooden slavery than to suffer
The flesh-fly blow my mouth. Hear my soul speak:
The very instant that I saw you, did
My heart fly to your service; there resides,
To make me slave to it; and for your sake
Am I this patient log-man.

Mir.   Do you love me?

Fer. O heaven, O earth, bear witness to this sound,
And crown what I profess with kind event,
If I speak true! if hollowly, invert   70
What best is boded me to mischief! I,
Beyond all limit of what else i' the world,
Do love, prize, honour you.

Mir.   I am a fool
To weep at what I am glad of.

Pros.   Fair encounter
Of two most rare affections! Heavens rain grace
On that which breeds between 'em!

Fer.   Wherefore weep you?

Mir. At mine unworthiness, that dare not offer
What I desire to give; and much less take
What I shall die to want. But this is trifling;
And all the more it seeks to hide itself,   80

The bigger bulk it shows. Hence, bashful cunning!
And prompt me, plain and holy innocence!
I am your wife, if you will marry me;
If not, I'll die your maid: to be your fellow
You may deny me; but I'll be your servant,
Whether you will or no.

Fer.   My mistress, dearest;
And I thus humble ever.

Mir.   My husband, then?

Fer.   Ay, with a heart as willing
As bondage e'er of freedom: here's my hand.

Mir.   And mine, with my heart in 't: and now farewell   90
Till half an hour hence.

Fer.   A thousand thousand!
                    [*Exeunt Fer. and Mir. severally.*

Pros. So glad of this as they I cannot be,
Who are surprised withal; but my rejoicing
At nothing can be more. I'll to my book;
For yet, ere supper-time, must I perform
Much business appertaining!   [*Exit.*

SCENE II

Another part of the Island.

Caliban, Stephano, and Trinculo.

Ste.   Tell not me;—when the butt is out, we will
drink water; not a drop before: therefore
bear up, and board 'em. Servant-monster,
drink to me.

Trin. Servant-monster! the folly of this island!
They say there's but five upon this isle: we

are three of them; if the other two be brained
like us, the state totters.

Ste. Drink, servant-monster, when I bid thee: thy
eyes are almost set in thy head.   10

Trin. Where should they be set else? he were a
brave monster indeed, if they were set in his
tail.

Ste. My man-monster hath drown'd his tongue in
sack: for my part, the sea cannot drown me;
I swam, ere I could recover the shore, five-and-
thirty leagues off and on. By this light, thou
shalt be my lieutenant, monster, or my standard.

Trin. Your lieutenant, if you list; he's no
standard.   20

Ste. We'll not run, Monsieur Monster.

Trin. Nor go neither; but you'll lie, like dogs, and
yet say nothing neither.

Ste. Moon-calf, speak once in thy life, if thou beest
a good moon-calf.

Cal. How does thy honour? Let me lick thy shoe.
I'll not serve him, he is not valiant.

Trin. Thou liest, most ignorant monster: I am in
case to justle a constable. Why, thou deboshed
fish, thou, was there ever man a coward that   30
hath drunk so much sack as I to-day? Wilt
thou tell a monstrous lie, being but half a fish
and half a monster?

Cal. Lo, how he mocks me! wilt thou let him, my
lord?

Trin. 'Lord,' quoth he! That a monster should be
such a natural!

Cal. Lo, lo, again! bite him to death, I prithee.

Ste. Trinculo, keep a good tongue in your head: if
you prove a mutineer,—the next tree! The   40

poor monster's my subject, and he shall not
suffer indignity.

Cal. I thank my noble lord. Wilt thou be pleased
to hearken once again to the suit I made to
thee?

Ste. Marry, will I: kneel and repeat it; I will stand,
and so shall Trinculo.

Enter Ariel, invisible.

Cal. As I told thee before, I am subject to a tyrant,
a sorcerer, that by his cunning hath cheated me
of the island.   50

Ari. Thou liest.

Cal. Thou liest, thou jesting monkey, thou:
I would my valiant master would destroy thee!
I do not lie.

Ste. Trinculo, if you trouble him any more in 's tale,
by this hand, I will supplant some of your
teeth.

Trin. Why, I said nothing.

Ste. Mum, then, and no more. Proceed.

Cal. I say, by sorcery he got this isle;   60
From me he got it. If thy greatness will
Revenge it on him,—for I know thou darest,
But this thing dare not,—

Ste. That's most certain.

Cal. Thou shalt be lord of it, and I'll serve thee.

Ste. How now shall this be compassed? Canst thou
bring me to the party?

Cal. Yea, yea, my lord: I'll yield him thee asleep,
Where thou mayst knock a nail into his head.

Ari. Thou liest; thou canst not.   70

Cal. What a pied ninny's this! Thou scurvy patch!

I do beseech thy greatness, give him blows,
And take his bottle from him: when that's gone,
He shall drink nought but brine; for I'll not show him
Where the quick freshes are.

Ste. Trinculo, run into no further danger: interrupt
the monster one word further, and, by this
hand, I'll turn my mercy out o' doors, and
make a stock-fish of thee.

Trin. Why, what did I? I did nothing. I'll go   80
farther off.

Ste. Didst thou not say he lied?

Ari. Thou liest.

Ste. Do I so? take thou that. [*Beats him*]
As you like this, give me the lie another time.

Trin. I did not give the lie. Out o' your wits,
and hearing too? A pox o' your bottle! this
can sack and drinking do. A murrain on your
monster, and the devil take your fingers!

Cal. Ha, ha, ha!   90

Ste. Now, forward with your tale.—Prithee, stand
farther off.

Cal. Beat him enough: after a little time,
I'll beat him too.

Ste.   Stand farther.—Come, proceed.

Cal. Why, as I told thee, 'tis a custom with him
I' th' afternoon to sleep: there thou mayst brain him,
Having first seized his books; or with a log
Batter his skull, or paunch him with a stake,
Or cut his wezand with thy knife. Remember
First to possess his books; for without them   100
He's but a sot, as I am, nor hath not
One spirit to command: they all do hate him
As rootedly as I. Burn but his books.
He has brave utensils,—for so he calls them,—

Which, when he has a house, he'll deck withal.
And that most deeply to consider is
The beauty of his daughter; he himself
Calls her a nonpareil: I never saw a woman,
But only Sycorax my dam and she;
But she as far surpasseth Sycorax   110
As great'st does least.

Ste.   Is it so brave a lass?

Cal. Ay, lord; she will become thy bed, I warrant,
And bring thee forth brave brood.

Ste. Monster, I will kill this man: his daughter
and I will be king and queen,—save our graces!
—and Trinculo and thyself shall be viceroys.
Dost thou like the plot, Trinculo?

Trin. Excellent.

Ste. Give me thy hand: I am sorry I beat thee;
but, while thou livest, keep a good tongue in   120
thy head.

Cal. Within this half hour will he be asleep:
Wilt thou destroy him then?

Ste.   Ay, on mine honour.

Ari. This will I tell my master.

Cal. Thou makest me merry; I am full of pleasure:
Let us be jocund: will you troll the catch
You taught me but while-ere?

Ste. At thy request, monster, I will do reason, any
reason.—Come on, Trinculo, let us sing.   [*Sings.*
                    Flout 'em and scout 'em,   130
                And scout 'em and flout 'em;
                    Thought is free.

Cal. That's not the tune.
                [*Ariel plays the tune on a tabor and pipe.*

Ste. What is this same?

Trin. This is the tune of our catch, played by the
picture of Nobody.

Ste. If thou beest a man, show thyself in thy likeness:
if thou beest a devil, take 't as thou list.

Trin. O, forgive me my sins!

Ste. He that dies pays all debts: I defy thee. Mercy   140
upon us!

Cal. Art thou afeard?

Ste. No, monster, not I.

Cal. Be not afeard; the isle is full of noises,
Sounds and sweet airs, that give delight, and hurt not.
Sometimes a thousand twangling instruments
Will hum about mine ears; and sometime voices,
That, if I then had waked after long sleep,
Will make me sleep again: and then, in dreaming,
The clouds methought would open, and show riches   150
Ready to drop upon me; that, when I waked,
I cried to dream again.

Ste. This will prove a brave kingdom to me, where
I shall have my music for nothing.

Cal. When Prospero is destroyed.

Ste. That shall be by and by: I remember the story.

Trin. The sound is going away; let's follow it,
and after do our work.

Ste. Lead, monster; we'll follow. I would I
could see this taborer; he lays it on.   160

Trin. Wilt come? I'll follow, Stephano.   [*Exeunt.*

81

SCENE III

Another part of the island.

*Enter Alonso, Sebastian, Antony, Gonzalo,
Adrian, Francisco, and others.*

Gon. By 'r lakin, I can go no further, sir;
My old bones ache: here's a maze trod, indeed,
Through forth-rights and meanders! By your patience,
I needs must rest me.

Alon.   Old lord, I cannot blame thee,
Who am myself attach'd with weariness,
To the dulling of my spirits: sit down, and rest.
Even here I will put off my hope, and keep it
No longer for my flatterer: he is drown'd
Whom thus we stray to find; and the sea mocks
Our frustrate search on land. Well, let him go.   10

Ant. [*Aside to Seb.*] I am right glad that he's so out of hope.
Do not, for one repulse, forego the purpose
That you resolved to effect.

Seb.   [*Aside to Ant.*] The next advantage
Will we take throughly.

Ant.   [*Aside to Seb.*] Let it be to-night;
For, now they are oppress'd with travel, they
Will not, nor cannot, use such vigilance
As when they are fresh.

Seb.   [*Aside to Ant.*] I say, to-night: no more.
                                        [*Solemn and strange music.*

Alon. What harmony is this?—My good friends, hark!

Gon. Marvellous sweet music!

*Enter Prospero above, invisible. Enter several strange Shapes,
bringing in a banquet: they dance about it with gentle actions
of salutation; and inviting the King, &c. to eat, they depart.*

Alon. Give us kind keepers, heavens!—What were these?   20

Seb. A living drollery. Now I will believe
That there are unicorns; that in Arabia
There is one tree, the phoenix' throne; one phoenix
At this hour reigning there.

Ant.   I'll believe both;
And what does else want credit, come to me,
And I'll be sworn 'tis true: travellers ne'er did lie,
Though fools at home condemn 'em.

Gon.   If in Naples
I should report this now, would they believe me?
If I should say, I saw such islanders,—
For, certes, these are people of the island,—   30
Who, though they are of monstrous shape,
           yet, note,
Their manners are more gentle-kind than of
Our human generation you shall find
Many, nay, almost any.

Pros.   [*Aside*] Honest lord,
Thou hast said well; for some of you there present
Are worse than devils.

Alon.   I cannot too much muse
Such shapes, such gesture, and such sound,
           expressing—
Although they want the use of tongue—a kind
Of excellent dumb discourse.

Pros.   [*Aside*] Praise in departing.

Fran. They vanish'd strangely.

Seb.   No matter, since   40
They have left their viands behind; for we have
          stomachs.—
Will 't please you taste of what is here?

Alon.   Not I.

Gon. Faith, sir, you need not fear. When we were boys,
Who would believe that there were mountaineers
Dew-lapp'd like bulls, whose throats had hanging
           at 'em

Wallets of flesh? or that there were such men
Whose heads stood in their breasts? which now
        we find
Each putter-out of five for one will bring us
Good warrant of.

Alon.   I will stand to, and feed,
Although my last: no matter, since I feel   50
The best is past. Brother, my lord the duke,
Stand to, and do as we.

*Thunder and lightning. Enter Ariel, like a harpy; claps
his wings upon the table; and, with a quaint device,
the banquet vanishes.*

Ari.   You are three men of sin, whom Destiny,—
That hath to instrument this lower world
And what is in 't,—the never-surfeited sea
Hath caused to belch up you; and on this island,
Where man doth not inhabit,—you 'mongst men
Being most unfit to live. I have made you mad;
And even with such-like valour men hang and drown
Their proper selves.

          [Alon., Seb. &c. draw their swords.

               You fools! I and my fellows   60
Are ministers of Fate: the elements,
Of whom your swords are tempered, may as well
Wound the loud winds, or with bemock'd-at stabs
Kill the still-closing waters, as diminish
One dowle that's in my plume: my fellow-ministers
Are like invulnerable. If you could hurt,
Your swords are now too massy for your strengths,
And will not be uplifted. But remember,—
For that's my business to you,—that you three
From Milan did supplant good Prospero;   70
Exposed unto the sea, which hath requit it,
Him and his innocent child: for which foul deed
The powers, delaying, not forgetting, have
Incensed the seas and shores, yea, all the creatures,
Against your peace. Thee of thy son, Alonso,
They have bereft; and do pronounce by me:

Lingering perdition—worse than any death
Can be at once—shall step by step attend
You and your ways; whose wraths to guard you
      from,—
Which here, in this most desolate isle, else falls 80
Upon your heads,—is nothing but heart-sorrow
And a clear life ensuing.

He vanishes in thunder; then, to soft music, enter the
Shapes again, and dance, with mocks and mows, and
carrying out the table.

Pros. Bravely the figure of this harpy hast thou
Perform'd, my Ariel; a grace it had, devouring:
Of my instruction hast thou nothing bated
In what thou hadst to say: so, with good life
And observation strange, my meaner ministers
Their several kinds have done. My high charms work,
And these mine enemies are all knit up
In their distractions: they now are in my power; 90
And in these fits I leave them, while I visit
Young Ferdinand,—whom they suppose is drown'd,—
And his and mine loved darling. [*Exit above.*

Gon. I' the name of something holy, sir, why stand you
In this strange stare?

Alon.   O it is monstrous, monstrous!
Methought the billows spoke, and told me of it;
The winds did sing it to me; and the thunder,
That deep and dreadful organ-pipe, pronounced
The name of Prosper: it did bass my trespass.
Therefore my son i' th' ooze is bedded; and 100
I'll seek him deeper than e'er plummet sounded,
And with him there lie mudded. [*Exit.*

Seb.   But one fiend at a time,
I'll fight their legions o'er.

Ant.   I'll be thy second.
                     [*Exeunt Seb. and Ant.*

Gon.　All three of them are desperate: their great guilt,
Like poison given to work a great time after,
Now 'gins to bite the spirits. I do beseech you,
That are of suppler joints, follow them swiftly,
And hinder them from what this ecstasy
May now provoke them to.

Adr.　　　　　　　　　　Follow, I pray you.　　[*Exeunt.*

ACT FOURTH
SCENE I

Before Prospero's cell.

Enter Prospero, Ferdinand, and Miranda.

Pros.　If I have too austerely punish'd you,
Your compensation makes amends; for I
Have given you here a third of mine own life,
Or that for which I live; who once again
I tender to thy hand: all thy vexations
Were but my trials of thy love, and thou
Hast strangely stood the test: here, afore Heaven,
I ratify this my rich gift. O Ferdinand,
Do not smile at me that I boast her off,
For thou shalt find she will outstrip all praise,　　10
And make it halt behind her.

Fer.　　　　　　　　　　I do believe it
Against an oracle.

Pros.　Then, as my gift, and thine own acquisition
Worthily purchased, take my daughter: but
If thou dost break her virgin-knot before
All sanctimonious ceremonies may
With full and holy rite be minister'd,
No sweet aspersion shall the heavens let fall
To make this contract grow; but barren hate,
Sour-eyed disdain and discord shall bestrew　　20

86

The union of your bed with weeds so loathly
That you shall hate it both: therefore take heed,
As Hymen's lamps shall light you.

Fer.   As I hope
For quiet days, fair issue and long life,
With such love as 'tis now, the murkiest den,
The most opportune place, the strong'st suggestion
Our worser genius can, shall never melt
Mine honour into lust, to take away
The edge of that day's celebration
When I shall think, or Phoebus' steeds are founder'd,   30
Or Night kept chain'd below.

Pros.   Fairly spoke.
Sit, then, and talk with her; she is thine own.
What, Ariel! my industrious servant, Ariel!

Enter Ariel.

Ari.   What would my potent master? here I am.

Pros.   Thou and thy meaner fellows your last service
Did worthily perform; and I must use you
In such another trick. Go bring the rabble,
O'er whom I give thee power, here to this place:
Incite them to quick motion; for I must
Bestow upon the eyes of this young couple   40
Some vanity of mine art: it is my promise,
And they expect it from me.

Ari.   Presently?

Pros.   Ay, with a twink.

Ari.   Before you can say, 'come,' and 'go',
And breathe twice, and cry, 'so, so,'
Each one, tripping on his toe,
Will be here with mop and mow.
Do you love me, master? no?

Pros.   Dearly, my delicate Ariel. Do not approach
Till thou dost hear me call.

Ari.   Well, I conceive.   [*Exit.*   50

Pros.   Look thou be true; do not give dalliance
Too much the rein: the strongest oaths are straw
To the fire i' the blood: be more abstemious,
Or else, good night your vow!

Fer.   I warrant you, sir;
The white cold virgin snow upon my heart
Abates the ardour of my liver.

Pros.   Well.
Now come, my Ariel! bring a corollary,
Rather than want a spirit: appear, and pertly!
No tongue! all eyes! be silent.   *[Soft music.*

Enter Iris.

Iris.   Ceres, most bounteous lady, thy rich leas   60
Of wheat, rye, barley, vetches, oats, and pease;
Thy turfy mountains, where live nibbling sheep,
And flat meads thatch'd with stover, them to keep;
Thy banks with pioned and twilled brims,
Which spongy April at thy hest betrims,
To make cold nymphs chaste crowns; and thy
          broom-groves,
Whose shadow the dismissed bachelor loves,
Being lass-lorn; thy pole-clipt vineyard;
And thy sea-marge, sterile and rocky-hard,
Where thou thyself dost air;—the queen o' the sky,   70
Whose watery arch and messenger am I,
Bids thee leave these; and with her sovereign grace,
Here on this grass-plot, in this very place,
To come and sport:—her peacocks fly amain:
Approach, rich Ceres, her to entertain.

Enter Ceres.

Cer.   Hail, many-colour'd messenger, that ne'er
Dost disobey the wife of Jupiter;
Who, with thy saffron wings, upon my flowers
Diffusest honey-drops, refreshing showers;
And with each end of thy blue bow dost crown   80
My bosky acres and my unshrubb'd down,
Rich scarf to my proud earth;—why hath thy queen
Summoned me hither, to this short-grass'd green?

Iris.   A contract of true love to celebrate;
       And some donation freely to estate
       On the blest lovers.

Cer.   Tell me, heavenly bow,
       If Venus or her son, as thou dost know,
       Do now attend the queen? Since they did plot
       The means that dusky Dis my daughter got,
       Her and her blind boy's scandal'd company   90
       I have forsworn.

Iris.   Of her society
       Be not afraid: I met her deity
       Cutting the clouds towards Paphos, and her son
       Dove-drawn with her. Here thought they to have done
       Some wanton charm upon this man and maid,
       Whose vows are, that no bed-right shall be paid
       Till Hymen's torch be lighted: but in vain;
       Mars's hot minion is return'd again;
       Her waspish-headed son has broke his arrows,
       Swears he will shoot no more, but play with sparrows,   100
       And be a boy right out.

Cer.   High'st queen of state,
       Great Juno, comes; I know her by her gait.

Enter Juno.

Juno.   How does my bounteous sister? Go with me
       To bless this twain, that they may prosperous be,
       And honour'd in their issue.   *[They sing.*

Juno.   Honour, riches, marriage-blessing,
       Long continuance, and increasing,
       Hourly joys be still upon you!
       Juno sings her blessings on you.

Cer.   Earth's increase, foison plenty,   110
       Barns and garners never empty;
       Vines with clustering bunches growing;
       Plants with goodly burthen bowing;
       Spring come to you at the farthest
       In the very end of harvest!

| | Scarcity and want shall shun you; |
| | Ceres' blessing so is on you. |

Fer. This is a most majestic vision, and
Harmonious charmingly. May I be bold
To think these spirits?

Pros.   Spirits, which by mine art   120
I have from their confines call'd to enact
My present fancies.

Fer.   Let me live here ever;
So rare a wonder'd father and a wise
Makes this place Paradise.

> [*Juno and Ceres whisper, and send Iris
> on employment.*

Pros.   Sweet, now, silence!
Juno and Ceres whisper seriously;
There's something else to do: hush, and be mute,
Or else our spell is marr'd.

Iris. You nymphs, call'd Naiads, of the windring brooks,
With your sedged crowns and ever-harmless looks,
Leave your crisp channels, and on this green land   130
Answer your summons; Juno does command:
Come, temperate nymphs, and help to celebrate
A contract of true love; be not too late.

Enter certain Nymphs.

You sunburn'd sicklemen, of August weary,
Come hither from the furrow, and be merry:
Make holiday; your rye-straw hats put on,
And these fresh nymphs encounter every one
In country footing.

*Enter certain Reapers, properly habited: they join with
the Nymphs in a graceful dance; towards the end whereof
Prospero starts suddenly, and speaks; after which, to a
strange, hollow, and confused noise, they heavily vanish.*

Pros. [*Aside*] I had forgot that foul conspiracy
Of the beast Caliban and his confederates   140

90

Against my life: the minute of their plot
Is almost come. [*To the Spirits*] *Well done!*
      avoid; no more!

Fer.   This is strange: your father's in some passion
       That works him strongly.

Mir.   Never till this day
       Saw I him touch'd with anger so distemper'd.

Pros.   You do look, my son, in a moved sort,
       As if you were dismay'd: be cheerful, sir.
       Our revels now are ended. These our actors,
       As I foretold you, were all spirits, and
       Are melted into air, into thin air: 150
       And, like the baseless fabric of this vision,
       The cloud-capp'd towers, the gorgeous palaces,
       The solemn temples, the great globe itself,
       Yea, all which it inherit, shall dissolve,
       And, like this insubstantial pageant faded,
       Leave not a rack behind. We are such stuff
       As dreams are made on; and our little life
       Is rounded with a sleep. Sir, I am vex'd;
       Bear with my weakness; my old brain is troubled:
       Be not disturbed with my infirmity: 160
       If you be pleased, retire into my cell,
       And there repose: a turn or two I'll walk,
       To still my beating mind.

Fer. Mir.   We wish your peace.   [*Exeunt.*

Pros.   Come with a thought. I thank thee, Ariel: come.

Enter Ariel.

Ari.   Thy thoughts I cleave to. What's thy pleasure?

Pros.   Spirit,
       We must prepare to meet with Caliban.

Ari.   Ay, my commander: when I presented Ceres,
       I thought to have told thee of it; but I fear'd
       Lest I might anger thee.

Pros.   Say again, where didst thou leave these varlets?   170

Ari. I told you, sir, they were red-hot with drinking;
So full of valour that they smote the air
For breathing in their faces; beat the ground
For kissing of their feet; yet always bending
Towards their project. Then I beat my tabor;
At which, like unback'd colts, they prick'd their ears,
Advanced their eyelids, lifted up their noses
As they smelt music: so I charm'd their ears,
That, calf-like, they my lowing follow'd through
Tooth'd briers, sharp furzes, pricking goss, and thorns,   180
Which enter'd their frail shins: at last I left them
I' the filthy-mantled pool beyond your cell,
There dancing up to the chins, that the foul lake
O'erstunk their feet.

Pros.   This was well done, my bird.
Thy shape invisible retain thou still:
The trumpery in my house, go bring it hither,
For stale to catch these thieves.

Ari.   I go, I go.   [*Exit.*

Pros. A devil, a born devil, on whose nature
Nurture can never stick; on whom my pains,
Humanely taken, all, all lost, quite lost;   190
And as with age his body uglier grows,
So his mind cankers. I will plague them all,
Even to roaring.

Re-enter Ariel, loaden with glistering apparel, &c.

                    Come, hang them on this line.

Prospero and Ariel remain, invisible.
Enter Caliban, Stephano, and Trinculo, all wet.

Cal. Pray you, tread softly, that the blind mole may not
Hear a foot fall: we now are near his cell.

Ste. Monster, your fairy, which you say is a harmless
fairy, has done little better than played the Jack with us.

Trin. Monster, I do smell all horse-piss; at which
my nose is in great indignation.   200

Ste. So is mine. Do you hear, monster? If I should
      take a displeasure against you, look you,—

Trin. Thou wert but a lost monster.

Cal. Good my lord, give me thy favour still.
      Be patient, for the prize I'll bring thee to
      Shall hoodwink this mischance: therefore speak softly.
      All's hush'd as midnight yet.

Trin. Ay, but to lose our bottles in the pool,—

Ste. There is not only disgrace and dishonour in
      that, monster, but an infinite loss.   210

Trin. That's more to me than my wetting: yet this
      is your harmless fairy, monster.

Ste. I will fetch off my bottle, though I be o'er ears
      for my labour.

Cal. Prithee, my king, be quiet. See'st thou here,
      This is the mouth o' the cell: no noise, and enter.
      Do that good mischief which may make this island
      Thine own for ever, and I, thy Caliban,
      For aye thy foot-licker.

Ste. Give me thy hand. I do begin to have bloody
      thoughts.   220

Trin. O King Stephano! O peer! O worthy
      Stephano! look what a wardrobe here is for thee!

Cal. Let it alone, thou fool; it is but trash.

Trin. O, ho, monster! we know what belongs to
      a frippery. O King Stephano!

Ste. Put off that gown, Trinculo; by this hand, I'll
      have that gown.

Trin. Thy grace shall have it.

Cal. The dropsy drown this fool! what do you mean   230
      To dote thus on such luggage? Let's alone,
      And do the murder first: if he awake,
      From toe to crown he'll fill our skins with pinches,
      Make us strange stuff.

93

Ste. Be you quiet, monster. Mistress line, is not
this my jerkin? Now is the jerkin under the
line: now, jerkin, thou are like to lose your hair,
and prove a bald jerkin.

Trin. Do, do: we steal by line and level, an 't like
your grace.   240

Ste. I thank thee for that jest; here's a garment
for 't: wit shall not go unrewarded while I am
king of this country. 'Steal by line and level'
is an excellent pass of pate; there's another
garment for 't.

Trin. Monster, come, put some lime upon your
fingers, and away with the rest.

Cal. I will have none on 't: we shall lose our time,
And all be turn'd to barnacles, or to apes
With foreheads villanous low.   250

Ste. Monster, lay-to your fingers: help to bear this
away where my hogshead of wine is, or I'll
turn you out of my kingdom: go to, carry this.

Trin. And this.

Ste. Ay, and this.

*A noise of hunters heard. Enter divers Spirits, in shape
of dogs and hounds, hunting them about; Prospero and
Ariel setting them on.*

Pros. Hey, Mountain, hey!

Ari. Silver! there it goes, Silver!

Pros. Fury, Fury! there, Tyrant, there! hark, hark!
                              [*Cal., Ste., and Trin. are driven out.*
        Go charge my goblins that they grind their joints
        With dry convulsions; shorten up their sinews   260
        With aged cramps; and more pinch-spotted make
                them
        Than pard or cat o' mountain.

Ari.   Hark, they roar!

Pros. Let them be hunted soundly. At this hour
Lie at my mercy all mine enemies:
Shortly shall all my labours end, and thou
Shalt have the air at freedom: for a little
Follow, and do me service.   [*Exeunt..*

ACT FIFTH
SCENE I

Before the cell of Prospero.

Enter Prospero in his magic robes, and Ariel.

Pros. Now does my project gather to a head:
My charms crack not; my spirits obey; and time
Goes upright with his carriage. How's the day?

Ari. On the sixth hour; at which time, my lord,
You said our work should cease.

Pros.   I did say so,
When first I raised the tempest. Say, my spirit,
How fares the king and 's followers?

Ari.   Confined together
In the same fashion as you gave in charge,
Just as you left them; all prisoners, sir,
In the line-grove which weather-fends your cell;   10
They cannot budge till your release. The king,
His brother, and yours, abide all three distracted,
And the remainder mourning over them,
Brimful of sorrow and dismay; but chiefly
Him that you term'd, sir, 'The good old lord,
          Gonzalo';
His tears run down his beard, like winter's drops
From eaves of reeds. Your charm so strongly
          works 'em,
That if you now beheld them, your affections
Would become tender.

Pros.   Dost thou think so, spirit?

Ari.   Mine would, sir, were I human.

Pros.   And mine shall.   20
Hast thou, which art but air, a touch, a feeling
Of their afflictions, and shall not myself,
One of their kind, that relish all as sharply,
Passion as they, be kindlier moved than thou art?
Though with their high wrongs I am struck to
          the quick,
Yet with my nobler reason 'gainst my fury
Do I take part: the rarer action is
In virtue than in vengeance: they being penitent,
The sole drift of my purpose doth extend
Not a frown further. Go release them, Ariel: 30
My charms I'll break, their senses I'll restore,
And they shall be themselves.

Ari.   I'll fetch them, sir.   [*Exit.*

Pros.   Ye elves of hills, brooks, standing lakes, and
          groves;
And ye that on the sands with printless foot
Do chase the ebbing Neptune, and do fly him
When he comes back; you demi-puppets that
By moonshine do the green sour ringlets make,
Whereof the ewe not bites; and you whose pastime
Is to make midnight mushrooms, that rejoice
To hear the solemn curfew; by whose aid—   40
Weak masters though ye be—I have bedimm'd
The noontide sun, call'd forth the mutinous winds,
And 'twixt the green sea and the azured vault
Set roaring war: to the dread rattling thunder
Have I given fire, and rifted Jove's stout oak
With his own bolt; the strong-based promontory
Have I made shake, and by the spurs pluck'd up
The pine and cedar: graves at my command
Have waked their sleepers, oped, and let 'em forth
By my so potent art. But this rough magic   50
I here abjure; and, when I have required
Some heavenly music,—which even now I do,—

To work mine end upon their senses, that
This airy charm is for, I'll break my staff,
Bury it certain fathoms in the earth,
And deeper than did ever plummet sound
I'll drown my book.   [*Solemn music.*

*Re-enter Ariel before: then Alonso, with a frantic gesture,
attended by Gonzalo; Sebastian and Antonio in like manner,
attended by Adrian and Francisco: they all enter the circle
which Prospero had made, and there stand charmed; which
Prospero observing, speaks:*

A solemn air, and the best comforter
To an unsettled fancy, cure thy brains,
Now useless, boil'd within thy skull! There stand,   60
For you are spell-stopp'd.
Holy Gonzalo, honourable man,
Mine eyes, even sociable to the show of thine,
Fall fellowly drops. The charm dissolves apace;
And as the morning steals upon the night,
Melting the darkness, so their rising senses
Begin to chase the ignorant fumes that mantle
Their clearer reason. O good Gonzalo,
My true preserver, and a loyal sir
To him thou follow'st! I will pay thy graces   70
Home both in word and deed. Most cruelly
Didst thou, Alonso, use me and my daughter:
Thy brother was a furtherer in the act.
Thou art pinch'd for 't now, Sebastian. Flesh and
                    blood,
You, brother mine, that entertain'd ambition,
Expell'd remorse and nature; who, with Sebastian,—
Whose inward pinches therefore are most strong,—
Would here have kill'd your king; I do forgive thee,
Unnatural though thou art. Their understanding
Begins to swell; and the approaching tide   80
Will shortly fill the reasonable shore,
That now lies foul and muddy. Not one of them
That yet looks on me, or would know me: Ariel,
Fetch me the hat and rapier in my cell:
I will disease me, and myself present

97

As I was sometime Milan: quickly, spirit;
Thou shalt ere long be free.

Ariel sings and helps to attire him.

        Where the bee sucks, there suck I:
        In a cowslip's bell I lie;
        There I couch when owls do cry.   90
        On the bat's back I do fly
        After summer merrily.
        Merrily, merrily shall I live now
        Under the blossom that hangs on the bough.

Pros.   Why, that's my dainty Ariel! I shall miss thee;
But yet thou shalt have freedom: so, so, so.
To the king's ship, invisible as thou art:
There shalt thou find the mariners asleep
Under the hatches; the master and the boatswain
Being awake, enforce them to this place,   100
And presently, I prithee.

Ari.   I drink the air before me, and return
Or ere your pulse twice beat.   *[Exit.*

Gon.   All torment, trouble, wonder and amazement
Inhabits here: some heavenly power guide us
Out of this fearful country!

Pros.   Behold, sir king,
The wronged Duke of Milan, Prospero:
For more assurance that a living prince
Does now speak to thee, I embrace thy body;
And to thee and thy company I bid   110
A hearty welcome.

Alon.   Whether thou be'st he or no,
Or some enchanted trifle to abuse me,
As late I have been, I not know: thy pulse
Beats, as of flesh and blood; and, since I saw thee,
The affliction of my mind amends, with which,
I fear, a madness held me: this must crave—
An if this be at all—a most strange story.
Thy dukedom I resign, and do entreat
Thou pardon me my wrongs.—But how should

     Prospero
    Be living and be here?

Pros.   First, noble friend,   120
    Let me embrace thine age, whose honour cannot
    Be measured or confined.

Gon.   Whether this be
    Or be not, I'll not swear.

Pros.   You do yet taste
    Some subtilties o' the isle, that will not let you
    Believe things certain. Welcome, my friends all!
    [*Aside to Seb. and Ant.*] But you, my brace of
        lords, were I so minded,
    I here could pluck his highness' frown upon you,
    And justify you traitors: at this time
    I will tell no tales.

Seb.   [*Aside*] The devil speaks in him.

Pros.   No.
    For you, most wicked sir, whom to call brother 130
    Would even infect my mouth, I do forgive
    Thy rankest fault,—all of them; and require
    My dukedom of thee, which perforce, I know,
    Thou must restore.

Alon.   If thou be'st Prospero,
    Give us particulars of thy preservation;
    How thou hast met us here, who three hours since
    Were wreck'd upon this shore; where I have lost—
    How sharp the point of this remembrance is!—
    My dear son Ferdinand.

Pros.   I am woe for 't, sir.

Alon. Irreparable is the loss; and patience   140
    Says it is past her cure.

Pros.   I rather think
    You have not sought her help, of whose soft grace
    For the like loss I have her sovereign aid,
    And rest myself content.

Alon.   You the like loss!

Pros. As great to me as late; and, supportable
         To make the dear loss, have I means much weaker
         Than you may call to comfort you, for I
         Have lost my daughter.

Alon.   A daughter?
         O heavens, that they were living both in Naples,
         The king and queen there! that they were, I wish   150
         Myself were mudded in that oozy bed
         Where my son lies. When did you lose your
                   daughter?

Pros. In this last tempest. I perceive, these lords
         At this encounter do so much admire,
         That they devour their reason, and scarce think
         Their eyes do offices of truth, their words
         Are natural breath: but, howsoe'er you have
         Been justled from your senses, know for certain
         That I am Prospero, and that very duke
         Which was thrust forth of Milan; who most strangely   160
         Upon this shore, where you were wreck'd, was
                   landed,
         To be the lord on 't. No more yet of this;
         For 'tis a chronicle of day by day,
         Not a relation for a breakfast, nor
         Befitting this first meeting. Welcome, sir;
         This cell's my court: here have I few attendants,
         And subjects none abroad: pray you, look in.
         My dukedom since you have given me again,
         I will requite you with as good a thing;
         At least bring forth a wonder, to content ye   170
         As much as me my dukedom.

*Here Prospero discovers Ferdinand and Miranda
playing at chess.*

   Mir. Sweet lord, you play me false.

   Fer.   No, my dear'st love,
         I would not for the world.

Mir.   Yes, for a score of kingdoms you should wrangle,
And I would call it fair play.

Alon.   If this prove
A vision of the island, one dear son
Shall I twice lose.

Seb.   A most high miracle!

Fer.   Though the seas threaten, they are merciful;
I have cursed them without cause.   *[Kneels.*

Alon.   Now all the blessings
Of a glad father compass thee about!   180
Arise, and say how thou camest here.

Mir.   O, wonder!
How many goodly creatures are there here!
How beauteous mankind is! O brave new world,
That has such people in 't!

Pros.   'Tis new to thee.

Alon.   What is this maid with whom thou wast at play?
Your eld'st acquaintance cannot be three hours:
Is she the goddess that hath sever'd us,
And brought us thus together?

Fer.   Sir, she is mortal;
But by immortal Providence she's mine:
I chose her when I could not ask my father   190
For his advice, nor thought I had one. She
Is daughter to this famous Duke of Milan,
Of whom so often I have heard renown,
But never saw before; of whom I have
Received a second life; and second father
This lady makes him to me.

Alon.   I am hers:
But, O, how oddly will it sound that I
Must ask my child forgiveness!

Pros.   There, sir, stop:
Let us not burthen our remembrances with
A heaviness that's gone.

Gon.   I have inly wept,   200
Or should have spoke ere this. Look down,
    you gods,
And on this couple drop a blessed crown!
For it is you that have chalk'd forth the way
Which brought us hither.

Alon.   I say, Amen, Gonzalo!

Gon.   Was Milan thrust from Milan, that his issue
Should become kings of Naples? O, rejoice
Beyond a common joy! and set it down
With gold on lasting pillars: In one voyage
Did Claribel her husband find at Tunis,
And Ferdinand, her brother, found a wife   210
Where he himself was lost, Prospero his dukedom
In a poor isle, and all of us ourselves
When no man was his own.

Alon.   [*To Fer. and Mir.*] Give me your hands:
Let grief and sorrow still embrace his heart
That doth not wish you joy!

Gon.   Be it so! Amen!

*Re-enter Ariel, with the Master and Boatswain
amazedly following.*

O, look, sir, look, sir! here is more of us:
I prophesied, if a gallows were on land,
This fellow could not drown. Now, blasphemy,
That swear'st grace o'erboard, not an oath on shore?
Hast thou no mouth by land? What is the news?   220

Boats. The best news is, that we have safely found
Our king and company; the next, our ship—
Which, but three glasses since, we gave out split—
Is tight and yare and bravely rigg'd, as when
We first put out to sea.

Ari.   [*Aside to Pros.*] Sir, all this service
Have I done since I went.

Pros.   [*Aside to Ari.*] My tricksy spirit!

Alon. These are not natural events; they strengthen
From strange to stranger. Say, how came you hither?

Boats. If I did think, sir, I were well awake,
I'ld strive to tell you. We were dead of sleep,   230
And—how we know not—all clapp'd under hatches;
Where, but even now, with strange and several noises
Of roaring, shrieking, howling, jingling chains,
And mo diversity of sounds, all horrible,
We were awaked; straightway, at liberty;
Where we, in all her trim, freshly beheld
Our royal, good, and gallant ship; our master
Capering to eye her:—on a trice, so please you,
Even in a dream, were we divided from them,
And were brought moping hither.

Ari.   [*Aside to Pros.*] Was 't well done?   240

Pros. [*Aside to Ari.*] Bravely, my diligence. Thou shalt be free.

Alon. This is as strange a maze as e'er men trod;
And there is in this business more than nature
Was ever conduct of: some oracle
Must rectify our knowledge.

Pros.   Sir, my liege,
Do not infest your mind with beating on
The strangeness of this business; at pick'd leisure
Which shall be shortly, single I'll resolve you,
Which to you shall seem probable, of every
These happen'd accidents; till when, be cheerful,   250
And think of each thing well. [*Aside to Ari.*] Come
                hither, spirit:
Set Caliban and his companions free;
Untie the spell. [*Exit Ariel.*] How fares my gracious
                sir?
There are yet missing of your company
Some few odd lads that you remember not.

Re-enter Ariel, driving in Caliban, Stephano, and
Trinculo, in their stolen apparel.

103

Ste. Every man shift for all the rest, and let no man
take care for himself; for all is but fortune.
—Coragio, bully-monster, coragio!

Trin. If these be true spies which I wear in my
head, here's a goodly sight. 260

Cal. O Setebos, these be brave spirits indeed!
How fine my master is! I am afraid
He will chastise me.

Seb. Ha, ha!
What things are these, my lord Antonio?
Will money buy 'em?

Ant. Very like; one of them
Is a plain fish, and, no doubt, marketable.

Pros. Mark but the badges of these men, my lords,
Then say if they be true. This mis-shapen knave,
His mother was a witch; and one so strong
That could control the moon, make flows and ebbs, 270
And deal in her command, without her power.
These three have robb'd me; and this demi-devil—
For he's a bastard one—had plotted with them
To take my life. Two of these fellows you
Must know and own; this thing of darkness I
Acknowledge mine.

Cal. I shall be pinch'd to death.

Alon. Is not this Stephano, my drunken butler?

Seb. He is drunk now: where had he wine?

Alon. And Trinculo is reeling ripe: where should they
Find this grand liquor that hath gilded 'em?— 280
How camest thou in this pickle?

Trin. I have been in such a pickle, since I saw you
last, that, I fear me, will never out of my bones:
I shall not fear fly-blowing.

Seb. Why, how now, Stephano!

Ste. O, touch me not;—I am not Stephano, but a cramp.

Pros. You'ld be king o' the isle, sirrah?

Ste. I should have been a sore one, then.

Alon. This is a strange thing as e'er I look'd on.

        [Pointing to Caliban.

Pros. He is as disproportion'd in his manners   290
  As in his shape. Go, sirrah, to my cell;
  Take with you your companions; as you look
  To have my pardon, trim it handsomely.

Cal. Ay, that I will; and I'll be wise hereafter,
  And seek for grace. What a thrice-double ass
  Was I, to take this drunkard for a god,
  And worship this dull fool!

Pros.   Go to; away!

Alon. Hence, and bestow your luggage where you found it.

Seb. Or stole it, rather.

      [Exeunt Cal., Ste., and Trin.

Pros. Sir, I invite your Highness and your train   300
  To my poor cell, where you shall take your rest
  For this one night; which, part of it, I'll waste
  With such discourse as, I not doubt, shall make it
  Go quick away: the story of my life,
  And the particular accidents gone by
  Since I came to this isle: and in the morn
  I'll bring you to your ship, and so to Naples,
  Where I have hope to see the nuptial
  Of these our dear-beloved solemnized;
  And thence retire me to my Milan, where   310
  Every third thought shall be my grave.

Alon.   I long
  To hear the story of your life, which must
  Take the ear strangely.

Pros.   I'll deliver all;
  And promise you calm seas, auspicious gales,
  And sail so expeditious, that shall catch

Your royal fleet far off. [*Aside to Ari.*] My
      Ariel, chick,
That is thy charge: then to the elements
Be free, and fare thou well! Please you, draw
      near.   [*Exeunt.*

EPILOGUE

Spoken by Prospero.

Now my charms are all o'erthrown,
And what strength I have's mine own,
Which is most faint: now, 'tis true,
I must be here confined by you,
Or sent to Naples. Let me not,
Since I have my dukedom got,
And pardon'd the deceiver, dwell
In this bare island by your spell;
But release me from my bands
With the help of your good hands: 10
Grentle breath of yours my sails
Must fill, or else my project fails,
Which was to please. Now I want
Spirits to enforce, art to enchant;
And my ending is despair,
Unless I be relieved by prayer,
Which pierces so, that it assaults
Mercy itself, and frees all faults.
As you from crimes would pardon'd be,
Let your indulgence set me free.   20

Glossary

A = on; II. i. 185.

ABUSE, deceive; V. i. 112.

ATCHËS (dissyllabic, pronounced 'aitches', like the letter H); I. ii. 370.

ADMIRE, wonder; V. i. 154.

ADVANCE, raise, lift up; I. ii. 408.

ADVENTURE, to risk: II. i. 187.

AFTER, afterwards; II. ii. 10.

AGAIN, again and again; I. ii. 390.

AGUE, a fever; II. ii. 68.

A-HOLD, 'to lay a ship a-hold', i.e. 'to bring a ship close to the wind so as to hold or keep her to it'; I. i. 52.

AMAZEMENT, anguish; I. ii. 14.

AMEN, used probably in the sense of 'again!' or perhaps merely with the force of 'many'; others render it 'hold, stop!' II. ii. 98.

AN, if; II. i. 181.

ANGLE, corner; I. ii. 223.

ARGIER, Algiers; I. ii. 261.

AS, as if; II. i. 121.

ASPERSION, sprinkling of rain or dew (with an allusion perhaps to the ceremony of sprinkling the marriage-bed with holy water); IV. i. 18.

ATTACHED, seized; III. iii. 5.

AVOID, begone; IV. i. 142.

BACKWARD, distant, past; I. ii. 50.

BADGES, 'household servants usually wore on their arms, as part of their livery, silver "badges" whereon the shield of their masters was engraved'; V. i. 267.

BAREFOOT (used adjectively); II. ii. 11.

BARNACLES, barnacle geese; IV. i. 249.

BASS, utter in a deep bass; III. iii. 99.

BAT-FOWLING, a term used for catching birds by night; thence the name of a thieves' trick for plundering shops about dusk by pretending to have lost a jewel near; II. i. 185.

BEAK, bow (of a ship); I. ii. 196.

BEAR UP, i.e. take your course, sail up; III. ii. 3.

BERMOOTHES, i.e. Bermudas; 'said and supposed to be inchanted and inhabited with witches and deuills, which grew by reason of accustomed monstrous thunder, storme, and tempest,' &c. Stows Annals; I. ii. 229.

BERRIES (? = Coffee); I. ii. 334.

BETID, happened; I. ii. 31.

BLUE-EYED, with dark circles around the eyes, taken to be a sign of pregnancy; I. ii. 269.

BOMBARD, a large-calibre cannon or a black tar-coated jug used for holding drink; II. ii. 21.

BOOTLESS, profitless; I. ii. 35.

BOSKY, wooded; IV. i. 81.

BOURN, boundary; II. i. 152.

BRAVE, fine; I. ii. 411.

BRING TO TRY, 'to lay the ship with her side close to the wind, and lash the tiller to the lee side'; I. i. 38.

BROOM-GROVES, groves in which broom (*Spartium scoparium*) abounds; or perhaps woods overgrown with *genista*, pathless woods; IV. i. 66.

BUDGE, stir; V. i. 11.

BULLY-MONSTER, a term of affection for a person; V. i. 258.

BURTHEN, undersong; I. ii. 381.

BUT, except that; I. ii. 414; otherwise than, I. ii. 119.

BY AND BY, immediately; III. ii. 156.

CAN, it able to make; IV. i. 27.

CANDIED, converted into sugar, sweetened; II. i. 279.

CAPABLE, retentive; I. ii. 353.

CAPERING, jumping for joy; V. i. 238.

CARRIAGE, burden; V. i. 3.

CASE, condition; III. ii. 29.

CAST, to throw up; perhaps with a play upon 'cast' in the sense of 'to assign their parts to actors'; II. i. 251.

CAT (with reference to the old proverb that good liquor will make a cat speak); II. ii. 86.

CATCH, a part-song; III. ii. 126.

CERTES, certainly; III. iii. 30.

CHALKED FORTH, i.e. chalked out; V. i. 303.

CHAPS, mouth; II. ii. 89.

CHERUBIN, a cherub; I. ii. 152.

CHIRURGEONLY, like a surgeon; II. i. 140.

CLEAR, blameless; III. iii. 82.

CLOSENESS, retirement; I. ii. 90.

CLOUDY, gloomy; II. i. 142.

COCKEREL, the young cock; II. i. 31.

COIL, turmoil; I. ii. 207.

COME BY, to acquire; II. i. 292.

CONFEDERATES, conspires; I. ii. 111.

CONSTANT, self-possessed; I. ii. 207; 'my stomach is not c.' i.e. 'is qualmish'; II. ii. 119.

CONTENT, desire, will; II. i. 269.

CONTROL, contradict; I. ii. 439.

CORAGIO, courage!; V. i. 258.

COROLLARY, a supernumerary, a surplus; IV. i. 57.

CORRESPONDENT, responsive, obedient; I. ii. 298.

COURSES, the larger lower sails of a ship; I. i. 52.

CRABBED, bad-tempered; III. i. 8.

CRABS, crab-apples; II. ii. 171.

CRACK, to burst (with reference to magic bands, or perhaps to the crucibles and alembics of magicians); V. i. 2.

DEAR, zealous; I. ii. 179.

DEAREST, most precious object; II. i. 135.

DEBOSHED, debauched; III. ii. 29.

DECKED, sprinkled; I. ii. 155.

DEEP, profound, wise; II. i. 266.

DELIVER, relate; V. i. 313.

DEMANDED, asked; I. ii. 139.

DEMI-PUPPETS, small elves; V. i. 36.

DEW-LAPPED, having flesh hanging from the throat (a reference probably to the victims of 'goitre'); III. iii. 45.

DIS, Pluto; IV. i. 89.

DISCASE, undress; V. i. 85.

DISCHARGE, performance, execution; used probably as a technical term of the stage; II. i. 254.

DISTEMPERED, excited; IV. i. 145.

DISTINCTLY, separately; I. ii. 200.

DOIT, the smallest piece of money; eighty doits went to a shilling; II. ii. 33.

DOLLAR, an English name for German and Spanish silver coins; II. i. 18.

DOWLE, a fibre of down; III. iii. 65.

DRAWN, having swords drawn; II. i. 308; having taken a good draught;
II. ii. 150.

DREGS (with reference to the liquor of the 'bombard', II. ii. 21–22);
II. ii. 42.

DROLLERY, puppet-show; III. iii. 21.

DRY, thirsty; I. ii. 112.

DULNESS, stupor; I. ii. 185.

EARTH'D, buried in the earth; II. i. 234.

EBBING, 'ebbing men', i.e. 'men whose fortunes are declining';
II. i. 226.

ECSTASY, mental excitement, madness; III. iii. 108.

ENDEAVOUR, laborious effort; II. i. 160.

ENGINE, instrument of war, military machine; II. i. 161.

ENTERTAINER, perhaps quibblingly interpreted by Gonzalo in the sense
of 'inn-keeper'; II. i. 17.

ENVY, malice; I. ii. 258.

ESTATE, to grant as a possession; IV. i. 85.

EYE, tinge; II. i. 55.

FALL, to let fall; II. i. 296.

FEARFUL, timorous; I. ii. 468.

FEATER, more becomingly; II. i. 273.

FEATLY, deftly; I. ii. 380.

FELLOWS, companions; II. i. 274.

FEW, 'in few', in few words, in short; I. ii. 144.

FILBERTS, hazel nuts; II. ii. 175.

FISH, to catch at, to seek to obtain; II. i. 104.

FLAT, low level ground; II. ii. 2.

FLAT-LONG, as if struck with the side of a sword instead of its edge;
II. i. 181.

FLESH-FLY, a fly that feeds on flesh and deposits her eggs in it;
III. i. 63.

FLOTE, flood, sea; I. ii. 234.

FOIL, disadvantage; III. i. 46.

FOISON, plenty; II. i. 163

FOOTING, dance; IV. i. 138.

FOUNDER'D, disabled by overriding, footsore; IV. i. 30.

FORTH-RIGHTS, straight paths; III. iii. 3.

FRAUGHTING, freighting: I. ii. 13.

FRESHES, springs of fresh water; III. ii. 75.

FRIPPERY, a place where old clothes are sold; IV. i. 225.

FRUSTRATE, frustrated; III. iii. 10.

FURZE, a prickly plant; I. i. 67.

GABERDINE, a long coarse outer garment; II. ii. 10.

GALLOWS, *cf.* 'He that is born to be hanged will never be drowned';
I. i. 32.

GARNERS, granaries; IV. i. 111.

GAVE OUT, i.e. gave up; V. i. 223.

GENTLE, high-born (and hence 'high-spirited'); I. ii. 468.

GILDED, made drunk (an allusion to the *aurum potabile* of the
alchemists); V. i. 280.

GINS, begins; III. iii. 106.

GLASSES, hour-glasses, i.e. runnings of the hour-glass; I. ii. 240.

GLUT, to swallow up; I. i. 63.

GOSS, nowadays gorse, a prickly plant, the same as 'furze'; IV. i. 180.

GRUDGE, murmur; I. ii. 249.

HEAVY, 'the heavy offer', i.e. the offer which brings drowsiness;
II. i. 194.

HELP, cure; II. ii. 97.

HESTS, behests; I. ii. 274.

HINT, theme; I. ii. 134; occasion, cause; II. i. 3.

HIS, its; II. i. 120.

HOIST, hoisted (past tense of 'hoise' or 'hoist'); I. ii. 148.

HOLLOWLY, insincerely; III. i. 70.

HOLP, helped; I. ii. 63.

HOME, to the utmost, effectively; V. i. 71.

HONEYCOMB, cells of honeycomb; I. ii. 329.

IGNORANT, appertaining to ignorance; 'i. fumes' = 'fumes of ignorance';
V. i. 67.

IMPERTINENT, irrelevant; I. ii. 138.

INCH-MEAL, inch by inch; II. ii. 3.

INFEST, vex; V. i. 246.

INFLUENCE (used in its astrological sense); I. ii. 182.

INFUSED, endowed; I. ii. 154.

INHERIT, take possession; II. ii. 179.

INLY, inwardly; V. i. 200.

INQUISITION, enquiry; I. ii. 35.

INVERT, change to the contrary; III. i. 70.

JACK, 'played the Jack,' i.e. the knave = 'deceived'; IV. i. 198.

JERKIN, a kind of doublet; IV. i. 236.

JUSTIFY, prove; V. i. 128.

KEY, tuning-key; I. ii. 83.

KIBE, heel-sore; II. i. 276.

KNOT (folded arms); I. ii. 224.

LAKIN, 'Ladykin', or the Virgin Mary; III. iii. 1.

LASS-LORN, forsaken by his lass; IV. i. 68.

LAUGHTER, possibly used with a double meaning; 'lafter' was perhaps the cant name of some small coin; still used provincially for the number of eggs laid by a hen at one time; II. i. 33.

LEARNING, teaching; I. ii. 366.

LETTERS, education and learning; II. i. 150.

LIEU, 'in lieu of', i.e. in consideration of; I. ii. 123.

LIFE, 'good life', i.e. 'life-like truthfulness'; III. iii. 86.

LIKE, similarly; III. iii. 66.

LIME, bird-lime; IV. i. 246.

LINE, lime-tree (with punning reference to other meanings of 'line' in subsequent portion of the scene); IV. i. 235.

LINE-GROVE, lime-grove; V. i. 10.

LIVER, regarded as the seat of passion; IV. i. 56.

LOATHNESS, reluctance; II. i. 130.

LORDED, made a lord; I. ii. 97.

LUSH, luscious, luxuriant; II. i. 52.

LUSTY, vigorous; II. i. 52.

MAID, maidservant or young woman; I. ii. 427.

MAIN-COURSE, the main sail; I. i. 38.

MAKE, to prove to be; II. i. 265.

MAKE A MAN, i.e. make a man's fortune; II. ii. 32.

MANAGE, government; I. ii. 70.

MARMOSET, small monkey; II. ii. 174.

MASSY, massive, heavy; III. iii. 67.

MATTER, an important matter; II. i. 230.

MEANDERS, winding paths; III. iii. 3.

MEASURE, pass over; II. i. 259.

MEDDLE, to mingle; I. ii. 22.

MERCHANT, merchantman ('the masters of some merchant'); II. i. 5.

MERELY, absolutely; I. i. 59.

METTLE, dispoution, ardour; II. i. 182.

MINION, favourite; IV. i. 98.

MIRACULOUS, 'the miraculous harp' of Amphion, the music of which raised the walls of Thebes; II. i. 86.

MISS, to do without; I. ii. 312; to fail in aiming at, not to hit; II. i. 40.

MO, more; II. i. 133.

MODESTY, virginity; III. i. 53.

MOMENTARY, instantaneous: I. ii. 202.

MOON-CALF, abortion; II. ii. 111.

MOP, grimace; IV. i. 47.

MORSEL, remnant, 'a piece of a man' (contemptuously); II. i. 286.

MOUNT, raise; II. ii. 11.

MOW, grimace: IV. i. 47.

MOW, make grimaces; II. ii. 9.

MUCH, 'to think it much', to reckon it as excessive, to grudge; I. ii. 252.

MUM, hush; III. ii. 59.

MUSE, wonder at; III. iii. 36.

NATURAL, idiot; III. ii. 37.

NATURE, natural affection; V. i. 76.

NEAT, horned beast: II. ii. 73.

NERVES, sinews; I. ii. 484.

NIMBLE, excitable; II. i. 173.

NINNY, simpleton; III. ii. 71.

NOBODY, an Elizatbethan sign; probably a direct allusion to the print of *No-body*, prefixed to the anonymous comedy of *No-body and Somebody* (printed before 1600) or to the engraving on the old ballad, called the *Well-Spoken Nobody*; III. ii. 136.

NOOK, bay; I. ii. 227.

NOTE, information; II. i. 248.

NOTHING, nonsense; II. i 170.

OBSERVATION, attention to detail; III. iii. 87.

OCCASION, critical opportunity; II. i. 207.

ODD, out-of-the-way; I. ii. 223.

O'ER, over again; 'trebles thee o'er', i.e. 'makes thee three times as great'; II. i. 221.

O'ERPRIZED, surpassed in value; I. ii. 92.

OF, as a consequence of; or = on, i.e. 'of sleep' = 'a-sleep'; V. i. 230.

OMIT, neglect; I. ii. 183; II. i. 194.

ON, of: I. ii. 87; IV. i. 157.

OOZE, bottom of the sea; I. ii. 252.

OR, ere, 'or ere' (a reduplication); I. ii. 11.

OUT, completely; I. ii. 41.

OVERBLOWN, blown over: II. ii. 114.

OVERTOPPING, outrunning; I. ii. 81.

OWED, owned; III. i. 45.

OWES, owns; I. ii. 407.

OWN, 'no man was his o.' i.e. 'master of himself, in his senses'; V. i. 213.

PAINFUL, laborious; III. i. 1.

PAINS, tasks; I. ii. 242.

PAPHOS, a city in Cyprus, one of the favourite seats of Venus; IV. i. 93.

PASS, thrust (a term of fencing), sally; IV. i. 244.

PASSION, suffering, grief; I. ii. 392.

PASSION, to feel pain or sorrow; V. i. 24.

PATCH, fool, jester; III. ii. 71.

PATE, 'pass of pate' = 'sally of wit'; IV. i. 244.

PAUNCH, run through the paunch; III. ii. 98.

PAY, repay; 'to pay home' = 'to repay to the utmost'; V. i. 70.

PERTLY, briskly; IV. i. 58.

PIECE, 'perfect specimen'; I. ii. 56.

PIED, motley-coated; III. ii. 71.

PIG-NUTS, earth-nuts; II. ii. 172.

PIONED AND TWILLED, of a stream, dug to keep it from silting and with the banks shored up with willow branches; IV. i. 64.

PLANTATION, colonisation; interpreted by Antonio in the ordinary sense; II. i. 143.

PLAY, act the part of; 'play the men', i.e. behave like men; I. i. 11.

POINT, detail; 'to point', in every detail; I. ii. 194.

POLE-CLIPT, with poles *clipt*, or embraced, by the vines; IV. i. 68.

POOR-JOHN, a cant name for hake salted and dried; II. ii. 28.

PRATE, endless chatter; II. i. 263.

PREMISES, conditions; I. ii. 123.

PRESENTED, represented; IV. i. 167.

PRESENTLY, immediately; I. ii. 125; IV. i. 42.

PROFESS, to make it one's business: II. i. 236.

PROFIT, to profit; I. ii. 172.

PROJECT, scheme, plan; II. i. 299.

PROVISION, foresight; I. ii. 28.

PURCHASED, acquired, won; IV. i. 14.

PUTTER-OUT, 'p. of five for one', one who invests, *puts out*, a sum of money before leaving home, on condition of receiving five times the amount on his return, i.e. 'at the rate of five for one'; III. iii. 48.

QUAINT, adroit, trim, excellent; I. ii. 317.

QUALITY, skill; I. ii. 193.

QUICK, living, fresh; III. ii. 75.

QUICKENS, gives life to; III. i. 6.

RABBLE, company, crowd (not used slightingly); IV. i. 37.

RACE, breed; I. ii. 358.

RACK, floating cloud; IV. i. 156.

RATE, estimation; I. ii. 92; reckoning; II. i. 109.

RAZORABLE, ready for shaving; II. i. 250.

REAR, raise; II. i. 295.

REASON, what is reasonable; III. ii. 128.

REASONABLE, 'reasonable shore', i.e. 'shore of reason'; V. i. 81.

RECOVER, restore; II. ii. 71, 79, 97.

REELING-RIPE, 'in a state of intoxication sufficiently advanced for reeling'; V. i. 279.

RELEASE, 'till your release' = till you release them; V. i. 11.

REMEMBER, commemorate; I. ii. 405; remind; I. ii. 243.

REMEMBRANCE, the faculty of remembering; II. i. 232.

REMORSE, pity; V. i. 76.

REQUIT, requited; III. iii. 71.

RESOLVE, explain to; V. i. 248.

RID, destroy; I. ii. 364.

ROOM, sea-room; I. i. 9.

ROUNDED, 'the whole round of life has its beginning and end in a sleep'; IV. i. 158.

SACK, a name applied to certain white wines of Spain; II. ii. 126.

SANCTIMONIOUS, holy; IV. i. 16.

SANS, without; I. ii. 97.

SCAMELS, probably some kind of bird, but not yet satisfactorily explained; II. ii. 176.

SCANDAL'D, scandalous; IV. i. 90.

SECURING, guarding; II. i. 310.

SEDGED, made of sedges; IV. i. 129.

SENSE, feelings; II. i. 107.

SENSIBLE, sensitive, II. i. 173.

SETEBOS, the god of Sycorax (said to be the chief god of the Patagonians); I. ii. 373; V. i. 261.

SETS OFF, i.e. shows to the best advantage; III. i. 2.

SEVERAL, separate; III. i. 42.

SHAK'D, shook; II. i. 319.

SHROUD, take shelter; II. ii. 42.

SIEGE, stool, excrement; II. ii. 110.

SIGNORIES, Italian states; I. ii. 71.

SINGLE, (1) solitary, (2) feeble; I. ii. 432.

SIRRAH, a form of 'sir', but it could be either respectful or demeaning, depending on the context; V. i. 291.

SOCIABLE, companionable, being in close sympathy; V. i. 63.

SOMETHING, somewhat; I. ii. 414.

SOMETIME, sometimes; I. ii. 198.

SORE (used quibblingly); V. i. 288.

SORT, possibly a punning allusion to 'sort' = 'lot'; II. i. 104.

SOT, fool; III. ii. 101.

SOUNDLY, thoroughly, smartly; II. ii. 81.

SOUTH-WEST, 'a south-west', i.e. a south-west wind (charged with the noxious breath of the Gulf-Stream); I. ii. 323.

SPEAK, to proclaim; II. i. 8.

SPHERE, orbit; II. i. 183.

SPONGY, soft ground; IV. i. 65.

SPOON, 'long spoon', an allusion to old proverb that 'he must have a long spoon that must eat with the devil'; II. ii. 103.

SPIRITING, the service done by a sprite; I. ii. 298.

STAIN, to disfigure; I. ii. 414.

STANDARD, standard-bearer, ensign; III. ii. 18; (quibble on 'standard' and 'stander'); III. ii. 19.

STANDING, 'standing water', i.e. water neither ebbing nor flowing; I. i. 221.

STEADED, stood in good stead; I. ii. 165.

STILL-CLOSING, constantly closing again; III. iii. 64.

STILL-VEXED, ever troubled; I. ii. 229.

STOCK-FISH, dried cod; III. ii. 79.

STOMACH, courage, I. ii. 157; appetite, inclination; II. i. 107.

STOVER, fodder for cattle; IV. i. 63.

STRANGE, rare; III. iii. 87.

STRANGELY, wonderfully; IV. i. 7.

STUDY, to give thought and attention to, to wonder; II. i. 81.

SUBSTITUTION, deputyship; I. ii. 103.

SUBTILTIES, the word 'subtilty' was borrowed from the language of
    cookery, and denoted a device in pastry, hence 'illusion'; V. i. 124.

SUDDEN, swift; II. i. 306.

SUFFERED, i.e. suffered death; II. ii. 38.

SUGGESTION, prompting, hint (*cf.* villainy); II. i. 288.

SURETY, guarantee; I. ii. 475.

SUSTAINING, bearing (them) up; I. ii. 218.

SWABBER, one who sweeps or *swabs* the deck of a ship; II. ii. 48.

TABOR, a small drum used for festivities; IV. i. 175.

TABORER, a player on a tabor; III. ii. 160.

TACKLE, ropes; I. ii. 147.

TALKING, saying; II. i. 96.

TANG, shrill sound; II. ii. 52.

TEEN, grief; I. ii. 64.

TASTE, experience; V. i. 123.

TELL, to count (the strokes of the clock); II. i. 15.

TEMPERANCE, temperature; Temperance, like Charity, used as a proper
    name; II. i. 42, 43.

TEMPORAL, practical activities in the external world; I. ii. 110.

TEND, attend; I. i. 6.

TENDER, to regard; II. i. 270.

THATCHED, covered, strewn; IV. i. 63.

THIRD = thrid, thread; IV. i. 3.

THROE, to cause pain; II. i. 231.

THROUGHLY, thoroughly; III. iii. 14.

TILTH, tillage; II. i. 152.

TO, for, as; II. i. 75; in comparison with; II. i. 178.

TRAFFIC, trade or commerce; II. i. 148.

TRASH, to check the speed of hounds when too forward; I. ii. 81.

TREBLES, 'tr. thee o'er,' i.e. 'makes thee thrice what thou art';
    II. i. 221.

TREMBLING, the '*tremor*' which is represented to be a sign of being possessed by the devil; II. ii. 83.

TRENCHER, a board on which food was served; II. ii. 187.

TRICE, 'on a tr.' i.e. 'in an instant'; V. i. 238.

TRICKSY, sportive; V. i. 226.

TRIFLE, phantom; V. i. 112.

TROLL, run glibly over (perhaps 'sing irregularly'); III. ii. 126.

TRUMPERY, gaudy costumes; IV. i. 186.

TURFY, grassy; IV. i. 62.

TWINK, a twinkling; IV. i. 43.

UNDER THE LINE, probably a term in tennis; 'to strike (the ball) under the line' = 'to lose the game'; IV. i. 236.

UNDERGOING, enduring; I. ii. 157.

UNICORN (with allusion to its proverbial ferocity); III. iii. 22.

UNSTANCHED, menstruating; I. i. 51.

UP-STARING, standing on end; I. ii. 213.

URCHINS, hedgehogs; hobgoblins; I. ii. 326.

URCHIN-SHOWS, elfin apparitions; II. ii. 5.

USE, to be accustomed; II. i. 175.

VANITY, illusion; IV. i. 41.

VARLETS, servants or rogues; IV. i. 170.

VAST, silent void, or vacancy (of night); I. ii. 327.

VERILY, true; II. i. 321.

VETCHES, fodder crops; IV. i. 61.

VIRGIN-KNOT, alluding to the girdle worn by maidens in ancient times; IV. i. 15.

VISITATION, affliction (as of a plague); III. i. 32.

VISITOR, priestly visitant, 'consolator'; II. i. 11.

VOUCHED, warranted; II. i. 60.

WAIST, the part of a ship between the quarter-deck and the forecastle; I. ii. 197.

WALLETS, flaps (of skin); III. iii. 46.

WARD, attitude of defence; I. ii. 471.

WEATHER, storm; I. i. 40.

WEATHER-FENDS, defends from the weather; V. i. 10.

WEIGHED, considered, pondered; II. i. 130.

WENCH (used as term of endearment); I. ii. 139, 412.

WEZAND, windpipe; III. ii. 99.

WHELP, a pup, but as a term of abuse (akin to the phrase 'son of a bitch'); I. ii. 283.

WHEN (an exclamation of impatience); I. ii. 316.

WHILE-ERE, short time since; III. ii. 127.

WHIST, hushed, silent; I. ii. 379.

WICKED, baneful; I. ii. 321.

WIDE-CHAPPED, opening the mouth wide; I. i. 60.

WINK, to close the eyes; II. i. 216.

WINK, the act of closing the eye, II. i. 285; (a short distance measured by a 'wink'; II. i. 242).

WISEST, 'after the wisest', i.e. 'in the wisest fashion'; II. ii. 77.

WOE, sorry; V. i. 139.

WORKS, affects; IV. i. 144.

WOUND, twined about; II. ii. 13.

WRANGLE, contend, quarrel; V. i. 174.

WRONG, 'to do oneself wrong', i.e. 'to be much mistaken'; I. ii. 443.

YARE, ready! I. i. 7; I. i. 37.

YARELY, alertly; I. i. 4.

YOND, there; I. ii. 409.

YOUR (= subjective genitive); V. i. 11.

ZENITH, the highest point of one's fortune; I. ii. 181.

Notes

I. i. 7–8. *'Take in the ... the master's whistle'* = Take down the upper sail [reducing the speed of the ship] and listen out for the master's whistle commands.

I. i. 22–25. *'You are a ... a rope more'* = You are a member of the king's privy council; if you can stop the storm and bring us calm weather, then we will stop working.

I. i. 28. *'mischance of the ... it so hap'* = the impending disaster, if it is to happen.

I. i. 31. *'drowning mark'* = the impression of someone likely to drown.

I. i. 32–34. *'Stand fast, / good ... destiny our cable'* = Fate, keep your focus on his hanging, and let his hanging rope be our anchor cable.

I. i. 55. *'What, must our mouths be cold?'* = What, must we die?

I. i. 60. *'The washing of ten tides!'* This expands on the theme of how the bodies of executed pirates were displayed by the shore to let three tides wash in and out over them.

I. i. 66–67. *'long heath, brown furze'*; so the folios; Hanmer's emendation has been generally accepted:—'ling, heath, broom, furze'.

I. i. 68. *'I would fain'* = I would be happy to.

I. ii. 4. *'welkin's cheek'* = the face of the sky.

I. ii. 23–24. *'Lend thy hand ... garment from me'* = Help me take off my magic cloak.

I. ii. 45–46. *'And rather like ... my remembrance warrants'* = It comes to me more like a dream than a clear memory.

I. ii. 50. *'In the dark ... abysm of time?'* = In the distant dark past, like an abyss.

I. ii. 72–73. *'being so reputed / In dignity'* = having such a respected reputation.

I. ii. 79–80. *'Being once perfected ... to deny them'* = Once he had perfected how to bestow favours or deny them.

I. ii. 81. *'To trash for over-topping'* = To stop them for being excessively ambitious.

I. ii. 81–82. *'new created ... that were mine'* = changed the loyalties of those who owed their position to me.

I. ii. 85–87. *'that now he ... verdure out on'* = He was like an ivy plant poisoning the health of the tree it was wrapped around.

I. ii. 92. *'O'er-prized all popular rate'* = I overestimated my value.

I. ii. 97. *'sans bound'* = without limit.

I. ii. 100–106. *'Who having into ... With all prerogative'* = Like a man who creates his own truth and make his memories into sinners, he came to believe he was the duke through his public activities, with all their outward authority.

I. ii. 121–122. *'being an enemy / To me inveterate'* = being an enemy of long standing.

I. ii. 146. *'carcass of a butt'* = shell of a boat.

I. ii. 156–157. *'which raised in me / An undergoing stomach'* = which gave me the resolution to survive.

I. ii. 169. *'Now I arise'*; probably derived from astrology; 'now my star is in the ascendant'; it should be noted that the stage direction 'Resumes his mantle' is not in the folios.

I. ii. 172–174. *'Have I, thy ... not so careful'* = I have ensured that you are better educated than other princesses, who have too much spare time and less diligent tutors.

I. ii. 181–184. *'I find my ... ever after droop'* = Through my knowledge of astrological arts I discern a favourable star, and I must act on this opportunity or my fortunes will deteriorate.

I. ii. 198. *'I flamed amazement'* = I amazed the onlookers with displays of fire. (He goes on to describe how he sent the flames along parts of the boat.)

I. ii. 202–203. *'more momentary / And sight-outrunning'* = fleeting and faster than they could follow with their eyes.

I. ii. 258–259. *'who with age ... into a hoop?'* = whose body was bent like a hoop through age and bitterness.

I. ii. 266. *'for one thing she did'*; Shakespeare does not tell us what he refers to here; perhaps he merely added the point in order to account for her preservation, or the incident may have been mentioned in his original.

I. ii. 281. *'As fast as mill-wheels strike'* = As fast as the blades of a watermill wheel strike the water.

I. ii. 326. *'pen thy breath up'* = catch your breath.

I. ii. 327. *'vast of night'* = the length of night.

I. ii. 329. *'As thick as honeycomb'* = As close together as the cells in a honeycomb.

I. ii. 352. *'Which any print ... wilt not take'* = You are incapable of receiving any form of goodness.

I. ii. 357–358. *'I endow'd thy ... made them known'* = I gave you the words to express your innermost thoughts.

I. ii. 378–379. *'Courtsied when you ... wild waves whist'* = Made a curtsey and blew a kiss [as performed before a country dance] to silence the waves.

I. ii. 385. *'The strain of strutting chanticleer'* = The crowing of a dominant cockerel.

I. ii. 408. *'The fringed curtains of thine eye advance'* = Open your eyes.

I. ii. 415. *'that's beauty's canker'* = the corrupter of beauty.

I. ii. 422–425. *'Vouchsafe my prayer ... bear me here'* = Grant my request to know whether you live on this island; and, more importantly, tell me how I should behave to ensure my survival.

I. ii. 433–434. *'He does hear ... does I weep'* = The King of Naples [now Ferdinand, implying Alonso's death] hears me, and so I weep.

I. ii. 451–452. *'I must uneasy ... the prize light'* = I must make winning her hand difficult, as he will not value her if her wins her too easily.

I. ii. 469. *'My foot my tutor?'* = Is my foot now in charge of my mind?

II. i. 5. *'The masters of some merchant'*; i.e. 'the owners of some merchantman'; Steevens suggested 'mistress' (old spelling 'maistres'); the Cambridge editors 'master's' (i.e. 'master's wife').

II. i. 8–9. *'weigh / Our sorrow with our comfort'* = balance our griefs with our pleasures.

II. i. 28. *'which, of he or Adrian'*; 'he' for 'him', used somewhat substantively, probably owing to the use of the word in the previous sentence, 'he will be talking.'

II. i. 36. The folios read: 'Seb. *Ha, ha, ha!* Ant. *So, you 're paid.*' Theobald gives the whole line to Sebastian; and his reading is adopted by the Camb. ed. Possibly a better emendation is the transposition of the prefixes to the speeches; the point of the quibble is no doubt the old proverb 'let them laugh that win.' Capell ingeniously suggested that the folio reading should stand with the slight change of 'you 've paid' for 'you 're paid'.

II. i. 60. *'As many vouched rarities are'* = As is the way with anything claimed to be rare.

II. i. 76. *'Not since widow Dido's time'*. A reference to the myth of Dido, Queen of Carthage, who lived with, and then was abandoned by, the Trojan prince Aeneas.

II. i. 86. *'miraculous harp'*. A reference to the magical lyre of Amphion, son of Zeus and Antiope.

II. i. 120–121. *'o'er his wave-worn ... to relieve him'* = the foot of the wave-eroded cliff seemed to bend over as if to help him.

II. i. 127. *'Who hath cause to wet the grief on 't.'* = Who has reason enough to cry tears of grief.

II. i. 128–129. *'importuned otherwise, / By all of us'* = We pleaded with you to act differently.

II. i. 130–131. *'Weigh'd between loathness … beam should bow'* = Choosing whether to fall on the side of unwillingness or obedience.

II. i. 143. *'Had I plantation of this isle'* = Were I to colonize this island.

II. i. 144. *'Or docks, or mallows'.* These are references to plants whose leaves soothe nettle stings.

II. i. 181. *'An it had not fallen flat-long'* = The joke fell flat (like the long, flat side of a sword instead of the cutting edge).

II. i. 182–184. *'You are gentlemen … weeks without changing.'* = [sarcastically] You are men of brave spirit. You would try to steal a full Moon if it stayed there for a period of five weeks.

II. i. 191–192. *'I wish mine … up my thoughts'* = I wish I could fall asleep and so close off my thoughts.

II. i. 216–217. *'wink'st / Whiles thou art waking.'* = You close your eyes (to this opportunity), while you are awake.

II. i. 222–223. *'to ebb / Hereditary sloth instructs me'* = Natural laziness causes me to pull back from opportunities.

II. i. 223–226. *'O, / If you … more invest it!'* = O, if you only knew how important you make the opportunity even as you mock it; how in stripping it of meaning you actually clothe it more meaningfully.

II. i. 226–228. *'Ebbing men, indeed … fear or sloth.'* = Unsuccessful men are often found at the bottom of the sea because of their caution or laziness.

II. i. 240–243. *'no hope that … doubt discovery there'* = You have no hope about one thing, but from a different perspective you now have a hope (of attaining the crown of Naples) that is so ambitious it can scarcely be seen, because its very possibility is in doubt.

II. i. 250. *'She that from whom'*; the unnecessary 'that' is perhaps intentionally repeated, owing to the previous repetition of 'she that'.

II. i. 265–266. *'I myself could … as deep chat'* = I could make a jackdaw talk like you chatter.

II. i. 266–268. *'O, that you … For your advancement!'* = If only you could see things like I do. This sleep offers you great fortunes.

II. i. 269–270. *'And how does … own good fortune?'* = How do you consider the possibilities to increase your own good fortune?

II. i. 279–280. *'candied be they … ere they molest!'* = they are coated in sugar and turn sticky before they affect me.

II. i. 285–287. *'To the perpetual ... upbraid our course'* = Once this aged man is put to death, he shall not rebuke us.

II. ii. 28–31. *'Were I in ... piece of silver'* = If I were in England, I'd put up a painted sign inviting people to gawp at Caliban and everyone would pay to do so.

II. ii. 38. *'hath lately suffered by a thunderbolt'* = was recently killed by lightning.

II. ii. 61. *'men of Ind'* = American Indians.

II. ii. 80. *'I will not take too much for him;'* i.e. 'I will take as much as I can possibly get.'

II. ii. 134. *'kiss the book'* = kiss the Bible or kiss a cup when raising a glass of drink to someone.

II. ii. 176. *'Scamels'*; not found elsewhere in Shakespeare. Many emendations have been made; staniel (a species of hawk) has been adopted by some editors; the word occurs probably in *Twelfth Night* (II. v. 124), though the editions read 'stallion'. 'Scamel' is evidently the name of a rock-breeding bird; Mr Wright has pointed out that, according to Stevenson's *Birds of Norfolk*, 'the female Bar-tailed Godwit is called a "Scamell" by the gunners of Blakeney.'

III. i. 1–2. *'There be some ... them sets off'* = There are some recreational activities that are painful, but their rewards outweigh their work.

III. i. 12–13. *'such baseness ... never like executor'* = such menial work was never done by one of such high social status.

III. i. 15. *'Most busy lest, when I do it;'* so the first folio. Various readings have been suggested; Pope, 'least busy when I do it'; Theobald, 'most busie-less when I do it'; Holt, 'most busiest, when I do it'; Spedding, 'most busiest when idlest', &c., &c. It seems likely that the reading of the second, third, and fourth folios throws light on the real meaning of the line:—'most busy least, when I do it'; i.e. 'most busy when I indulge my thoughts, least busy when I am actually at work'. A comma after 'busy' instead of after 'least' would simplify this reading, but it is possible to understand it as punctuated in the folios; Shakespeare probably wished to make the superlatives as antithetical as possible; perhaps we should read 'labour' for 'labours'.

III. i. 41–42. *'The harmony of ... too diligent ear'* = The beauty of their voices has enslaved my attention.

III. i. 52. *'how features are abroad'* = what foreign people look like.

III. ii. 79. *'make a stock-fish of thee'*. Dried fish was beaten before cooking to soften it.

III. ii. 98. *'paunch him with a stake'* = stab him in the guts.

III. ii. 112–113. *'she will become ... forth brave brood'* = she will become your wife, I'll bet, and give you a brood of handsome children.

III. ii. 128–129. *'I will do reason, any / reason'* = I will do anything within reason.

III. ii. 154. *'I shall have my music for nothing'* = I shall not pay the court musicians.

III. iii. 26. *'travellers ne'er did lie'*. Travellers' tales were honest in the sense that they had moved on before the truth of the stories could be checked.

III. iii. 39. *'Praise in departing'*; a proverbial expression: 'stay your praises till you see how your entertainment will end.'

III. iii. 47. *'Whose heads stood in their breasts'*. There were wild contemporary reports from foreign lands of strange men who had their faces in their chests.

III. iii. 48. *'putter-out of five for one'*. A reference to a method of financing exploration, in which explorers placed a deposit or investment before their voyage, and if they returned they would receive five times the original sum.

III. iii. 54–55. *'That hath ... is in 't'* = Fate uses this world to work out its schemes

III. iii. 55–56. *'never-surfeited sea ... belch you up'* = The sea has no limit to the numbers of men it will drown, but it still chose to throw them back to land.

III. iii. 61–65. *'the elements ... in my plume'* = The elements that have formed your swords may as well make futile attempts to wound the wind or stab water that closes up instantly as they might try to destroy the tiniest feather in my plumage.

III. iii. 102–103. *'But one fiend ... their legions o'er'* = I'll fight legions of spirits if they come at me one at a time.

IV. i. 3. *'a third of mine own life'* = i.e. Miranda.

IV. i. 25–28. *'With such love ... honour into lust'* = Based on the strength of our love, the darkest room, the most seductive setting, the strongest temptations of our based selves will never override my honour with lust.

IV. i. 51–52. *'do not give ... much the rein'* = Do not tempt yourselves too much through excessive flirting.

IV. i. 57–58. *'Now come, my ... want a spirit'* = Come, Ariel, bring one too many spirits rather than not enough.

IV. i. 64. *'pioned and twilled'*; dug (a stream) and shored up (its banks) with willow branches to prevent silting.

IV. i. 66. *'To make cold nymphs chaste crowns'* = To make innocent flower crowns for modest girls.

IV. i. 97. *'Till Hymen's torch be lighted'* = Until the wedding ceremony has taken place.

IV. i. 98. *'Mars's hot minion'* = Venus, the goddess of love and sexuality.

IV. i. 110. Mr Wright suggests that 'earth's' should be read as a dissyllable, 'earthes'; the second, third, and fourth folios read *'and'* before 'foison'.

IV. i. 114–115. *'Spring come to you ... end of harvest!'* = May spring arrive just after the harvest (i.e. skipping winter).

IV. i. 134–135. *'You sunburn'd sicklemen ... from the furrow'*. This is an injunction for the sunburned labourers in the field, harvesting with their sickles, to come in from the field.

IV. i. 147, &c. In *The Tragedies of Darius*, by William Alexander, afterwards Earl of Sterling, published in the year 1603, occurs the following passage, which, according to Steevens, may have been the original of Shakespeare's speech:—

> 'Let greatnesse of her glascie scepters vaunt:
> Not scepters, no, but reeds, soone brus'd, soone broken:
> And let this worldlie pomp our wits inchant.
> All fades, and scarcelie leaues behind a token.
> Those golden pallaces, those gorgeous halles,
> With fourniture superfluouslie faire:
> Those statelie courts, those sky-encountering walles
> Evanish all like vapours in the aire.'

IV. i. 151. *'baseless fabric of this vision'* = insubstantial nature of this spectacle.

IV. i. 176. *'unback'd colts'* = young horses that have not yet been trained to be ridden.

IV. i. 179. *'That, calf-like, they my lowing follow'd'* = That followed me like calves following their lowing mother.

IV. i. 193. The folios read 'hang on them'.

IV. i. 221. *'O King Stephano! O Peer!'* an allusion to the song, often referred to in Elizabethan literature, 'Take thy cloak about thee':—

> 'King Stephen was a worthy peere,
> His breeches cost him but a crowne,
> He held them sixpence all too deere;
> Therefore he called the taylor Lowne.'

The ballad is printed in Percy's *Reliques*; Shakespeare also quotes it in *Othello*, II. iii. 92.

IV. i. 231. *'Let's alone;'* some verb of motion must be understood, i.e. 'let us go alone' (leaving Trinculo behind); 'alone' is possibly an error of the folios for 'along', as suggested by Theobald.

IV. i. 237–238. *'thou are like ... a bald jerkin'*. This may be a reference to the belief that people lost their hair in the tropics.

IV. i. 239. *'we steal by line and level'* = we steal with precision (like the sailor uses a plumb line and the carpenter uses a level).

V. i. 2–3. *'time / Goes upright with his carriage'* = Time flows more freely, now that its load is lightened.

V. i. 21–24. *'Hast thou, which ... than thou art?'* = If you, an airy spirit, should have empathy for them, how can I, a human being like them, not be moved more?

V. i. 27–30. *'the rarer action ... a frown further'* = It is rarer to act with moral dignity than it is to unleash vengeance. If they are contrite, then I will not extend my anger any further.

V. i. 37. *'green sour ringlets'* = a ring of mushrooms in the grass, said to be a place where fairies danced.

V. i. 39. *'midnight mushrooms'* = mushrooms that spring up quickly during the night.

V. i. 43–44. *'And 'twixt the ... Set roaring war'* = Caused the sea and the sky to war against one another.

V. i. 58–60. *'A solemn air ... within thy skull!'* = A harmonious piece of music, the best way to settle an anxious imagination, may restore your mind, which is presently boiling in your skull.

V. i. 63. *'even sociable to the show of thine'* = sympathetic to what your own eyes express.

V. i. 70–71. *'I will pay ... word and deed'* = I will repay you in my words and actions.

V. i. 81–82. *'Will shortly fill ... foul and muddy'* = The clear tidal waters of understanding will soon cover the confused and polluted ignorance.

V. i. 112. *'Or some enchanted trifle to abuse me'* = Or some magical hallucination will deceive me.

V. i. 115. *'The affliction of my mind amends'* = My confused state is lifting.

V. i. 123–124. *'You do yet ... o' the isle'* = You are still under the influence of the uncanny illusions of the island.

V. i. 127–128. *'I here could ... justify you traitors'* = I could let the king's wrath descend upon you and brand you traitors.

V. i. 145–147. *'supportable / To make ... to comfort you'* = I can help you to endure your loss, although I have weaker means than the comfort you already have.

V. i. 174–175. *'Yes, for a ... it fair play.'* = You would play against me just for a few kingdoms, but such is my love I wouldn't mind.

V. i. 186. *'Your eld'st acquaintance cannot be three hours'* = You cannot have known her longer than three hours.

V. i. 198. *'Must ask my child forgiveness'.* Alonso must ask Miranda forgiveness for sending her to what he thought would be her death when she was an infant.

V. i. 219. *'That swear'st grace o'erboard, not an oath on shore'* = You who by swearing made God's grace abandon our ship.

V. i. 236. *'Where we, in all her trim, freshly beheld'* = When we first saw the ship in an undamaged condition.

V. i. 243–244. *'And there is ... ever conduct of'* = In this affair there are powers other than nature at play.

V. i. 247. *'at pick'd leisure'* = at a moment of your choosing.

V. i. 248–250. *'single I'll resolve ... These happen'd accidents'* = In private I will give you a plausible explanation of these events.

V. i. 256. *'Every man shift for all the rest'* = Every man make space for the other.

V. i. 271. *'And deal in ... without her power'* = And use the Moon's power without its permission.

V. i. 309. The line is to be read, according to the folios, 'to see our dear belov'd solémnizéd.'

V. i. 311. *'Every third thought shall be my grave'* = A third of my thinking will be reflection on attaining a good life.

Epilogue. 16–18. *'Unless I be ... frees all faults'* = Unless I am freed by a mercy that pleads before God and forgives my sins.

WILLIAM SHAKESPEARE –
HIS LIFE AND TIMES.

We have few details of Shakespeare's personal life, and some of these are disputed, but we can trace his life in theatre with some confidence. This was a man who learned his craft; insisted on fair remuneration; found (and retained) royal favour and escaped political snares. Aligned with one company, he could write with specific actors in mind and experiment as different theatres offered new staging possibilities. His creativity was impacted only by frequent outbreaks of plague, which closed the theatres.

1557

John Shakespeare marries Mary Arden. The couple may have known each other since childhood; his father farmed land owned by her father.

26 APRIL 1564

The couple's third child, William, is baptized. His date of birth is not known, and the day usually celebrated – 23 April, or Saint George's Day – appeals only because this is known to be the day of his death, in 1616. That said, baptism was expected during this period to take place no later than seven days after birth.

EDUCATION

William is probably educated at the King's New School in Stratford-upon-Avon, about a quarter-mile from his home.

At this time, a grammar school education involves principally the teaching of Latin (with some Greek), preparing boys for careers in the civil service. The art of rhetoric teaches them how to communicate with an audience, learning the importance of delivery and gesture.

Boys also study classical poetry and drama, and write their own compositions, in both English and Latin or Greek. They perform these in front of their class – and sometimes perform plays on holidays.

JULY 1575, KENILWORTH

The Earl of Leicester's Men, a major acting company, perform *The Delivery of the Lady of the Lake* at Kenilworth Castle. Crowds flock to their performances, from 9 to 27 July, and it is possible that William is among them. A reference to 'Arion on the dolphin's back' in *Twelfth Night* (I. ii. 15) may reflect his familiarity with the classical tale, but it may also echo a particularly noteworthy spectacle: musicians performing inside a dolphin.

27 NOVEMBER 1582

A marriage licence is issued to William, then aged 18, and Anne Hathaway, then aged 26. It's probable the marriage is one of necessity: permission is granted to read the marriage banns only once (not the usual three times) and a daughter, Susanna, is baptized less than six months later, on 26 May 1583.

2 FEBRUARY 1585

Twins, son Hamnet and daughter Judith, are baptized.

1585–1592, THE 'LOST YEARS'

William disappears from the historical record, and we do not know how he supports his young family during this time. Is he a schoolmaster? A legal clerk? A soldier?

At some point in the late 1880s, he arrives in London. Perhaps to avoid prosecution for poaching deer – though probably not. This and other stories arise in the years (and centuries) following his death, in part a response to misreading contemporary documents. 'Shakespeare' is a common enough name in the sixteenth century, and there is only one document that seems certain to refer to William: a 'complaints bill' for a case before the Queen's Bench between 1588 and 1589.

SHAKESPEARE, THE ACTOR

William begins his life in the theatre as an actor. This aspect of his life is often overlooked, not least because actors are held in low esteem during his lifetime – and, indeed, for many centuries after it.

Reform of the Poor Laws during Elizabeth's reign had made life for travelling companies particularly difficult. An act 'for the punishment of vagabondes' (1572) allowed for the arrest and imprisonment of the unemployed, and itinerant actors were often targeted. Acting companies therefore required the protection of theatrical sponsors such as the Earl of Leicester and the Earl of Sussex, whose playing company the young William joins.

Though never a star, he will act for 15 years – which suggests a certain skill. At a time when audiences are both loud and generous with their responses, a bad player will be hissed from the stage, their exit further encouraged by the lobbing of an orange or two. His first biographer, Nicolas Rowe, tells us that his role as the Ghost in *Hamlet* was 'the top of his performance'. William also appears in the cast list for several plays by Ben Jonson, including *Sejanus*, performed in 1603.

1589–1592, EARLY WRITING

Apparently recognizing that he does not excel as an actor, William finds a new role: he breathes new life into old and tired plays, collaborates with established dramatists and begins to write alone.

With others, he writes: *The Second Part of Henry the Sixth* (1591); *The Third Part of Henry the Sixth* (1591); *The Lamentable Tragedy of Titus Andronicus* (1592); and *The First Part of Henry the Sixth* (1592).

On his own, he writes the following plays (whose dates are difficult to establish with any certainty): *The Taming of the Shrew* (1589–1592); *The Two Gentleman of Verona* (1591–1592); and *King Richard the Third* (1592/4). Lord Strange's Men are associated with the first performance of this last play, and Lord Strange himself is a direct descendant of Thomas Stanley, a character in the play whose role is pivotal. William may be a member of the company.

1592, 'AN UPSTART CROW'

Robert Greene, a popular dramatist, publishes a pamphlet, *Greenes, Groats-worth of Witte, bought with a million of Repentance*. He has both a BA and an MA from Cambridge, and complains:

> there is an upstart Crow, beautified with our feathers, that with his Tygers hart wrapt in a Players hyde, supposes he is as well able to bombast out a blanke verse as the best of you: and being an absolute Johannes fac totum, is in his owne conceit the onely Shake-scene in a countrey.

This *Johannes fac totum* is a Jack of all trades – and, obviously, a master of none. Drama should clearly be left to university graduates, not actors.

Just six years later, however, another Cambridge graduate, the author Francis Meres, will write:

> As Plautus and Seneca are accounted the best for comedy and tragedy among the Latins, so Shakespeare among the English is the most excellent in both kinds for the stage.

Incidentally, the reference to 'his Tygers hart wrapt in a Players hyde' is an allusion to a line from *Henry VI, Part III* – which suggests the play had enjoyed considerable success.

1593–1594

Plague closes the theatres, and Lord Strange's Men leave London to tour. William writes two narrative poems, which prove popular and will be reprinted several times during his lifetime. He dedicates both to Henry Wriothesley, 3rd Earl of Southampton. The dedication for Venus and Adonis is brief – 'The love I dedicate to your Lordship is without end'; the dedication for *The Rape of Lucrèce* is extravagant:

> The love I dedicate to your lordship is without end ... What I have done is yours; what I have to do is yours; being part in all I have, devoted yours.

We do not know the nature of the relationship between the two men, and both dedications offer few clues – during this period, writers depend on their sponsors for support, political as well as financial. However, the Earl is often identified as the 'Fair Youth' of Shakespeare's sonnets: his celebrated looks and personality seem to match.

It's an identification that is disputed, not least because Henry is 39 (hardly a youth) when the sonnets are first published, in 1609 – though this is a collection written between 1593 and 1608.

1594, *THE COMEDY OF ERRORS*

William adapts *Menaechmi*, by Plautus – a play he may well have read at school. It is performed by 'a company of base and common fellows' at Gray's Inn Hall on 28 December 1594.

1594, THE LORD CHAMBERLAIN'S MEN

Many members of Lord Strange's Men leave to found this 'playing company', under the patronage of Henry Carey, 1st Baron Hunsdon and the Lord Chamberlain. It will become known as the King's Men in 1603, when the new king, James I, becomes patron.

Profits (and debts) are split between eight 'sharers', including William and Richard Burbage, who will become one of the most famous actors of his time and the first to play the roles of Hamlet, Othello, King Lear and Macbeth.

With this new arrangement, William effectively receives royalties for his work, at a time when writers are usually at the mercy of theatre managers, earning low prices and paid only according to the amount produced. In 1600, the impresario Philip Henslowe is paying £6–7 a play and the proceeds from one day's performance.

Originally the company performs at The Theatre, Shoreditch. On 29 December 1598, after difficulties with the landlord and a move to another theatre, The Theatre is dismantled overnight and carried south of the river to Southwark, where a new theatre is built: The Globe.

1595–1596

The Lord Chamberlain's Men have exclusive rights to perform William's plays, which gives him an unusual opportunity – to develop roles for and in collaboration with the actors.

• *Love's Labour's Lost*
Probably written around this time, the play is unusual for having no clear literary source while its pageants recall royal entertainments. (It will be performed in front of the Queen at Christmas, 1597.)
Does the play have a sequel, *Love's Labour's Won*? Francis Meres suggests as much, but it's not certain whether this is a play that has now been lost or is simply an alternative title to another play.

• *A Midsummer Night's Dream*
This may be the first play William writes for the Lord Chamberlain's Men – though the first certain date we have for its performance is 1604 at Hampton Court. Bottom may have been played by the great comic actor Will Kempe.

• *The Tragedy of Romeo and Juliet*
According to the First Quarto, published in 1597, this play 'hath been often (and with great applause) plaid publiquely' – which suggests it is an immediate success. Richard Burbage probably plays Romeo, and a misprint in the First Quarto suggests that Will Kempe plays Peter.

• *The Life and Death of King Richard the Second*
It's possible that William plays the role of John of Gaunt. The play is popular and will be printed three times by 1598.

11 AUGUST 1596

Son Hamnet is buried, dead from unknown causes at the age of 11.

1597–1598

Throughout his career, William moves between London and Stratford, where he buys New Place as his family home, in 1597. It is one of the largest properties in the town, which suggests he has enjoyed considerable financial success.

By 1598, he has also secured a reputation: his name is now a selling point and appears on the title pages of editions of his plays.

• *The Merchant of Venice*
Richard Burbage plays Shylock and Will Kempe plays Lancelot Gobbo, in a play described by Francis Meres and the First Folio as a comedy. It has been performed 'divers times' by 1600, the date of a first edition.

• *The First Part of Henry the Fourth*
The character we know now as Falstaff is originally called Oldcastle. This proves controversial: Oldcastle's descendants, the Lords Cobham, are powerful and take advantage when Henry Carey, the Lord Chamberlain, dies. The company is now 'piteously persecuted by the Lord Mayor and the aldermen', according to the contemporary playwright Thomas Nashe. Within the year, the appointment of Carey's son to Lord Chamberlain restores the company's protection, and Oldcastle is renamed Falstaff.

• *The Second Part of Henry the Fourth*
The epilogue thanks the audience and assures them that Sir John Falstaff will return in a new play. It also clarifies that Falstaff is not Oldcastle, who 'died martyr, and this is not the man'.

• *Much Ado About Nothing*
The most performed of Shakespeare's comedies, it is very popular in the years following its first performance. Will Kempe plays Dogberry, who will leave the company in 1599 – possibly because his talent for improvisation proves irritating. *Hamlet* (written within the next two years) includes this advice to the Players: 'And let those that play your clowns speak no more than is set down for them'.

1599

• *The Life of Henry the Fifth*
In the final act, Henry's triumphant return from London is compared to the Earl of Essex, soon to be 'from Ireland coming, / Bringing rebellion broached on his sword'. It's a confident prediction for the Queen's favourite, but by June England knows that his expedition has failed: the new play is already out of date.

• *As You Like It*
Scholars agree that this is the first play to be performed at the Globe. Tradition has it that William plays Adam, who may have written the role of Rosalind with a specific boy player in mind.

• *The Tragedy of Julius Caesar*
Richard Burbage plays the role of Brutus. Caesar is played by the actor John Heminges, who will be co-editor of the First Folio.

1600–1601

• *The Tragedy of Hamlet*
Richard Burbage is the first to play the Prince. Many believe that John Heminges plays Polonius, and that contemporary audiences laugh at the boastful line: 'I did enact Julius Caesar: I was killed i' the Capitol; Brutus killed me'.

• *The Merry Wives of Windsor*
A play that shows signs of having been written in haste. Biographer Nicolas Rowe insists that the Queen 'was so well pleased with that admirable character of *Falstaff*, in the two parts of *Henry the Fourth*, that she commanded him [Shakespeare] to continue it for one play more, and to shew him in love'. It's a story that has as many detractors as supporters.

• *Twelfth Night, or What You Will*
Whether or not this is commissioned to perform during Twelfth Night celebrations at Whitehall Palace in 1601, the comedy is written around this time. Robert Arnim has replaced Will Kempe as the leading comic actor, and William is now writing for him: Feste is a character who is no mere entertainer but shows a keen intelligence.

1603–1610

Repeated outbreaks of plague close theatres (for a total of 60 months – five full years), and William's output slows.

He collaborates several times with Thomas Middleton, who also contributes scenes to Macbeth, and with George Wilkins for *Pericles, Prince of Tyre* (1608). The Tragedy of Cymbeline (1610) also shows signs of collaboration.

In Thomas North's translation of *Plutarch's Lives* (first published in 1580, then expanded in 1595 and again in 1603), he finds inspiration for *The Tragedy of Antony and Cleopatra* (1607–1608) and *Coriolanus* (1605–1608). It's clear he also reads Plutarch's original Greek text closely.

There are no records of performances for *All's Well That Ends Well* (1605) or *The Life of Timon of Athens* (1605), which may never have been produced.

• *The Tragedy of Othello* (1604)
Richard Burbage plays the Moor. It is possible that Robert Arnim plays Iago: he was the actor most usually given songs, and Iago sings two drinking songs. The historical setting – the Turkish invasion of Cyprus, leading to the Battle of Lepanto – may be politically astute: a new monarch sits on the throne, James I, and he has recently written a poem about the battle.

• *Measure for Measure* (1604)
This may have been prompted by his research for Othello: an important source for both plays is Cinthio's Gli Hecatommithi.

• *The Tragedy of King Lear* (1605–1606)
Richard Arnim plays the Fool, a character who is no clown but who dares to criticize the king even as he remains loyal. Richard Burbage plays Lear, a story with contemporary echoes. In 1603, Sir Brian Annesley, a rich father of three daughters, had become senile. His two older daughters tried to take advantage to contest his will, knowing that his main beneficiary was their younger sister, Cordell.

• *The Tragedy of Macbeth* (1606)
Several details suggest strongly that this play was written in the aftermath of the Gunpowder Plot of 1605. The words 'fair' and 'foul' are the echoes of a sermon given by Lancelot Andrewes in front of the king; a medal struck to celebrate the plot's thwarting depicted a serpent hiding among flowers, echoing the advice given by Lady Macbeth: 'Look like the innocent flower, but be the serpent under't'.

1611

• *The Winter's Tale*
The play is based closely on *Pandosto*, by Robert Greene who had been so contemptuous of the 'upstart crow'. Staged at the Globe – the earliest performance recorded is May – it will be performed at Court in front of the King in November.

• *The Tempest*
This seems to have been written for staging at the Blackfriars playhouse, an indoor theatre owned by the company since 1608.

The characters who leave the stage at the end of Act IV are the same who return for Act V. This suggests an interval – probably to replace the candles and torches that provided lighting.

1612–1614

William now works with John Fletcher, who will eventually replace him as the company's playwright.

23 APRIL 1616

William dies. The cause is unknown and seems to have been unexpected; he had declared himself to be in 'perfect health' when preparing his will, barely a month earlier. Half a century later, John Ward, vicar of Stratford, will record the local gossip: 'Shakespeare, Drayton, and Ben Jonson had a merry meeting and, it seems, drank too hard, for Shakespeare died of a fever there contracted.'

Three King's Men receive bequests: Richard Burbage, John Heminges and Henry Condell.

13 MARCH 1619

Richard Burbage dies – and London mourns. 'He's gone and with him what a world are dead,' writes an anonymous poet, remembering 'Hamlet ... scant of breath', 'Tyrant Macbeth with unwash'd, bloody hand', and 'let me not forget one chiefest part, / Wherein, beyond the rest, he mov'd the heart; / The grieved Moor'.

1623, THE FIRST FOLIO

John Heminges and his fellow King's Man Henry Condell prepare and edit *Mr. William Shakespeare's Comedies, Histories, & Tragedies* for publication. Its significance cannot be underestimated: it is the only reliable text for about 20 plays, and the first publication for a further 18.

The preface tells us that a funerary monument has been erected at Holy Trinity Church, Stratford to honour William Shakespeare, a poet with the genius of Socrates and the art of Virgil: 'The earth buries him, the people mourn him, [Mount] Olympus possesses him'.